The Church of England
and
The Moravian Church in Great Britain and Ireland

ANGLICAN-MORAVIAN CONVERSATIONS

The Fetter Lane Common Statement

with

Essays in Anglican and Moravian History
by Colin Podmore

THE COUNCIL FOR CHRISTIAN UNITY
OF THE GENERAL SYNOD OF THE CHURCH OF ENGLAND

Council for Christian Unity
Occasional Paper No. 5

First published in 1996 by the Council for Christian Unity of the General Synod of the Church of England

COPYRIGHT

The copyright of *The Fetter Lane Common Statement* is held by the Co-Chairmen of the Conversations, the Rt Revd Peter Coleman and the Rt Revd Geoffrey Birtill.

The *Essays in Moravian and Anglican History* are copyright © The Central Board of Finance of the Church of England 1996.

Requests to reproduce extracts from the Common Statement or the Essays should be addressed to: The Copyright Manager, Central Board of Finance of the Church of England, Church House, Great Smith Street, London SW1P 3NZ.

It is not necessary to seek specific permission for the reproduction of extracts from *The Fetter Lane Common Statement* amounting to a total of not more than 500 words, providing that the copyright is appropriately acknowledged as shown below.

The Fetter Lane Common Statement is copyright © Peter Coleman and Geoffrey Birtill.

ISBN 0 7151 5751 5

Printed in England by Cromwell Press, Melksham, Wiltshire

The front cover incorporates the episcopal seal of the *Unitas Fratrum*.

CONTENTS

	Page
THE FETTER LANE COMMON STATEMENT	1
for contents see p. 2	
ESSAYS IN MORAVIAN AND ANGLICAN HISTORY	35
by Colin Podmore	
for contents see p. 36	
APPENDICES	83
for contents see p. 84	

THE FETTER LANE COMMON STATEMENT

Towards Visible Unity
between the Church of England and the
Moravian Church in Great Britain and Ireland

Text agreed following the final plenary meeting,
held at the
Fetter Lane Moravian Church, Chelsea, 19 May 1995

CONTENTS

		Page
FOREWORD by the Co-Chairmen		3
I	OUR SHARED PAST AND PRESENT	7
II	OUR COMMON CALLING TO FULL, VISIBLE UNITY	12
III	WHAT WE CAN NOW AGREE IN FAITH	17
IV	THE ORDAINED MINISTRY OF THE CHURCH	21
V	APOSTOLICITY AND SUCCESSION	25
VI	ISSUES STILL TO BE FACED	28
VII	OUR COMMON FUTURE	30
Participants in the Conversations		33

Biblical quotations are from the Revised Standard Version.

FOREWORD
by the Co Chairmen

1. The quest for Christian unity has long challenged Christian minds and consciences, but never more than in this century has the exploration towards unity been so vigorous and insistent. The twentieth-century world has itself become more of a global village than ever before and the need for interdependence and co-operation among nations has sharpened the minds of those who previously sheltered behind national boundaries to accept new horizons and larger loyalties. The churches have not been unaffected by this, although their motivation towards unity springs from the mandate from Christ himself who prayed that his followers might all be one. This century has witnessed unparalleled movements within the Christian churches to break down divisions and to enter into a deeper life of witness and commitment together. These are signs of a process of reaching out to each other from entrenched positions. While we may claim that the justification for this process is theological, we acknowledge that the imperative of effective mission is no less paramount. We recognize that we need to work together in our modern society to achieve credibility and to share both rich traditions and our limited resources in order to be more effective ambassadors of the Gospel.

2. The Moravian Church and the Church of England share common roots. Both our churches recognize that their origins lie in the Christian tradition of pre-Reformation Europe. We have inherited much that is common to both churches although historically and theologically the reformation experience led each to develop its insights and church life along different paths. Today both churches are also members of world-wide communions which transcend national boundaries and are a global expression of Christian unity which each has experienced separately. We are now seeking to move towards visible unity between our two different traditions within one national boundary.

3. It was for these reasons that in 1985 the Moravian Church approached the Church of England, suggesting the setting up of Conversations. After an initial exploratory meeting, it was agreed that Conversations should begin after the 1988 Lambeth Conference. From 1989 to 1995 our delegations met sixteen times for one-day or two-day

meetings, and this Common Statement is the result. It is named after the Fetter Lane Moravian Church in Chelsea, where we held our final meeting. This was felt to be particularly appropriate, since the Fetter Lane Society, from which that congregation is descended, began in 1738 as a society founded for Anglicans and others by a Moravian, Peter Böhler, and among whose membership were John Wesley and other future Methodist, Moravian and Anglican leaders who played a vital role in the Evangelical Revival.

4. These Conversations do not spring out of an ecumenical void, but are built upon a relationship that extends back to the Moravian Bishop Jan Amos Comenius in the seventeenth century and to Nicholas, Count Zinzendorf in the eighteenth century. More recently an Anglican-Moravian dialogue in England continued from 1878 to 1936, but the goals which they sought eluded those involved. Only in the last decade have they been revived. For detailed information on this see the Essay 'The *Unitas Fratrum* and the Church of England', appended to this Common Statement.

5. We hope that our work will not only bring our churches closer together in this country, but also serve as the basis for progress towards visible unity between Anglicans and Moravians in other countries where our traditions exist alongside each other. Furthermore, we hope that our work will also serve as a contribution to the wider ecumenical quest.

6. In preparing to draft our Common Statement it was clear that our first task was to learn more about each other, our understanding of ecclesiology, our policies on initiation and ministry, how we worked in our parishes and congregations. From that analysis we assessed what we had in common and what was distinct in belief, forms of government, orders of worship and in the exercise of teaching and pastoral ministry. We discovered from this what we can now agree in faith (Chapter 3).

7. Furthermore, we had to explore together what our fundamental ecumenical aim was in these Conversations. We shared the conviction that Christ's reconciling work and his prayer for his disciples 'that they may be one even as we are one' (John 17. 22) means that the ecumenical task has to be pursued until all the separated churches achieve *full visible unity*. On the way to that ultimate goal, we saw two interim stages, *visible unity between bilateral partners,* implying *inter alia* a reconciliation of

ministries, and where that is not yet achievable such *preliminary steps towards visible unity* as two churches can agree in good conscience.

8. Our Common Statement explores the preliminary steps we think possible now as the way towards a visible unity for the Church of England and the Moravian Church.

9. We realize that full visible unity between the major world-wide Christian communions is not to be expected soon. Nevertheless, crucial theological groundwork has been laid down in the report of the Faith and Order Commission of the World Council of Churches, *Baptism, Eucharist and Ministry,* the Meissen and Porvoo Common Statements and many of the ecumenical theological dialogues. The consensus we have reached in our Conversations is based upon this groundwork.

10. We have found that we share a common adherence to Scripture, common Creeds, the same dominical sacraments, and similar styles in our general structures of worship. We have looked carefully at our understanding of ministries as the area of faith and practice where real differences might be expected, and we set out what we can agree about ordained ministry in chapter 4, and about apostolic succession in chapter 5. We have not required of each other any compromise of the theological convictions we hold on these complex issues, nor have we always used traditional language. In our search together to find what we hold in common our original awareness of the particular and unique relationship between our two episcopal churches was strengthened. We discovered what we can confidently commend to our respective church members.

11. In moving towards visible unity, we have tried to be clear how such a move to unity could express the distinct ethos of each of our churches. We indicate in chapter 6 a model of communion with diversity, and identify issues where more convergence is needed before this can be fully achieved.

12. Finally, in chapter 7 we make a series of recommendations for our shared future which if accepted would enable us to make progress now towards visible unity between our two churches.

13. Our work has required quite detailed historical study, not all of which can be included in the Common Statement. We have added as appendices essays in Moravian and Anglican history prepared for us by

Dr Colin Podmore. We are grateful for his assiduous and expert help. Dr Mary Tanner has steered us through these Conversations with her masterly blend of wide theological discernment, immense Faith and Order experience, and practical wisdom. Without their help the preparation of this Statement would have been far more difficult.

GEOFFREY BIRTILL EP. FR. ✠ PETER CREDITON
The Rt Revd Geoffrey Birtill The Rt Revd Peter Coleman
Bishop of the *Unitas Fratrum* Bishop of Crediton

February 1996

I OUR SHARED PAST AND PRESENT

1. The Moravian Church and the Church of England inherit a history of contacts and fellowship stretching over more than three hundred years.[1] There are incidents in our common past which call for repentance, but our churches have never condemned each other, and have seen each other as 'sister churches',[2] each being among the oldest ecumenical partners of the other.

2. The *Unitas Fratrum* or Church of the Bohemian Brethren, of which the present-day Moravian Church is the continuation, was founded in 1457 by followers of the Czech reformer Jan Hus (c. 1372-1415), but was virtually extinguished in its homelands in the 1620s. From 1722 descendants of the *Unitas Fratrum* founded a new village, Herrnhut, on the estate of Count Nikolaus Ludwig von Zinzendorf (1700-1760) in Saxony. In 1727 Herrnhut's inhabitants had a pentecostal experience of the Holy Spirit which gave them a new sense of unity. Under Zinzendorf's leadership they became a Christian community which understood itself as a renewal of the *Unitas Fratrum,* and the international body into which it soon grew came to be known in English as the Moravian Church.[3]

3. In the 1640s Jan Amos Comenius (1592-1670), bishop-in-exile of the *Unitas Fratrum*, visited England and attempted to promote unity and reconciliation. In 1660 the episcopally-ordered Church of England was restored, but the *Unitas Fratrum*, reduced to a remnant now suffering persecution in its place of exile, was dying. Comenius bequeathed his church to the care of the Church of England, and in subsequent decades collections were encouraged in the Church of England on behalf of the Bohemian Brethren in exile. The consecration of the first bishops of the renewed *Unitas*

---

[1] For a fuller account of this history, see the essay 'The *Unitas Fratrum* and the Church of England' appended to this Common Statement.

[2] This phrase was used by Bishop Edmund Gibson of London in 1744. In 1737 Archbishop John Potter of Canterbury had described the Moravian Church as closer to the Church of England than any other, saying that the Moravians were 'our brethren, and one Church with our own'.

[3] For a fuller account, see the essays 'The Origins of our Churches: The Church of the Bohemian Brethren' and 'The Origins of our Churches: The Moravian Church', appended to this Common Statement.

Fratrum by Daniel Ernst Jablonski (1660-1741), one of the last bishops of the old *Unitas Fratrum*, in 1735 and 1737 was undertaken with a view to English recognition of Moravian orders, and the continuation and renewal of the *Unitas Fratrum* which it involved was warmly encouraged and welcomed by the then Archbishop of Canterbury, John Potter.

4. Like Comenius and Jablonski, Zinzendorf was a passionate worker for Christian unity. In 1746, four years after the establishment of the first Moravian congregations in England, Zinzendorf made proposals to Archbishop Potter whereby he hoped to enable Anglicans who joined the Moravian Church to enjoy Moravian worship and discipline without thereby separating from the Church of England. This proved impossible, however.

5. Comenius' account of the *Unitas Fratrum*'s church order had won the approval of Anglican divines in the 1660s, and in the 1730s and 1740s Anglican bishops repeatedly expressed esteem for the Moravian Church's apostolicity and, in particular, its style of episcopacy. The bench of bishops actively supported the Act of Parliament of 1749 which described the Moravian Church as 'an antient Protestant Episcopal Church'.

6. Since the beginning of the Moravian Church's overseas missions in 1732, Moravians' zeal for mission throughout the world and the Moravian Church's work and approach in the mission field have repeatedly won Anglican admiration. It was this admiration, coupled with a resulting desire for close co-operation, which produced and sustained efforts to achieve Anglican recognition of Moravian orders (and the resulting interchangeability of ministers) from 1878 onwards. By 1907 it became clear that a simple recognition was not possible,[4] so instead an attempt was made to agree a scheme for the gradual establishment of an interchangeable ministry. Discussions continued over a further period of thirty years, but failed to produce agreement on a wider vision of unity within which such an interchangeable ministry could be set.

7. The 1948 Lambeth Conference, accepting that the bilateral Anglican-Moravian conversations had at that stage run their natural course, expressed instead the hope that progress would be made through

---

[4] This was because, as the report of a committee appointed by the Archbishop of Canterbury said, the bishops of the Moravian Church did not stand in an unbroken tactile succession from those of the early Church: see the essays 'The Origins of our Churches: The Moravian Church' and 'The *Unitas Fratrum* and the Church of England'.

general Anglican conversations with the Free Churches. In England these conversations led to the proposed Covenant for Unity between the Church of England and the Methodist, Moravian and United Reformed Churches. The covenanting process enabled representatives of the Church of England and the Moravian Church to get to know each other and to become familiar with each other's ethos and traditions. In 1982, however, the General Synod of the Church of England was unable to endorse the Covenant with these three churches. The Moravian Church's Provincial Synod approved the Covenant proposals by a vote of 98% in favour.

8. In 1984 the Moravian Synod authorized the Provincial Board and the Faith and Order Committee to examine the possibility of further moves towards unity with other churches and enter into discussion with them if this seemed desirable. The Committee decided that it would be appropriate to approach the Church of England, and did so in February 1985. In response the General Synod's Standing Committee agreed to formal Conversations, which began in 1989.

Anglican-Moravian Relationships Today

9. Since 1982 our churches have continued to work together, in the Inter-Church process and the ecumenical instruments which it produced. We share a commitment to the Council of Churches for Britain and Ireland, Churches Together in England and many similar bodies at intermediate and local levels. Local congregations co-operate and exchange in many ways, and in Malmesbury Anglican and Moravian churches have covenanted together in a local ecumenical partnership.

10. In England many of the formulations of Moravian liturgy have been influenced by Anglican liturgical texts (Moravian worship nevertheless retains a distinctive ethos), while Anglicans have widely adopted the Moravian Christingle service. Each church sings hymns written by members of the other.

11. Our churches also have in common the fact that they both owe allegiances beyond these islands – the Moravian Church in Great Britain and Ireland is a province of the international *Unitas Fratrum*, while the Church of England belongs to the Anglican Communion. These two international bodies are different in character.[5]

---

[5] See 'The International Structures of our Churches', appended to this Common Statement.

12. The *Unitas Fratrum* is one single international church. Until the mid-nineteenth century it was highly centralized, but since then decision-making authority has gradually been devolved. Nevertheless, it retains a common Church Order, amended by resolutions of the Unity Synod, which meets every seven years. It is only within the framework set by this Church Order that each of the nineteen provinces is responsible for ordering its own life. Between the Unity Synods the Unity Board (consisting of one member from the Provincial Board of each of the Provinces governed by a Synod) has authority to act on behalf of the *Unitas Fratrum* in all matters which fall within the function of a Unity Synod.

13. The Anglican Communion, by contrast, is a communion of 32 self-governing member churches. The oldest member churches had been independent of each other for a century or more before the first Lambeth Conference of bishops met in 1867. More recently an Anglican Consultative Council (including bishops, clergy and laity) and a Primates' Meeting have been established. These structures, together with the ministry of the Archbishop of Canterbury, serve to bind in interdependence churches which are nevertheless juridically independent. Canons are made by the national, provincial or diocesan synods. The resolutions of the Lambeth Conference are not binding but have a moral authority by virtue of those gathered in Conference.

14. Both world bodies continue to develop, and as they do so a certain convergence can be identified. In the Anglican Consultative Council and the Primates' Meeting the Anglican Communion has created bodies in some way comparable in membership to the Unity Synod and the Unity Board, albeit without the decision-making authority of their Moravian counterparts. The international Moravian Bishops' Conference held in 1992 recommended that a Bishops' Conference be held every seven years, midway between meetings of the Unity Synod. This represented an attempt to give structural expression to the collegiality of Moravian bishops internationally, but without a status comparable to that of the Lambeth Conference within the Anglican Communion.

15. In some areas of the world Anglicans and Moravians co-operate particularly closely, and this has already led to Anglican bishops sharing

in the consecration of Moravian bishops in Tanzania, Alaska and England.[6]

16. This developing fellowship requires us now to set out an agreement on our churches' common calling to the goal of full, visible unity and the steps on the way to it. The recent ecumenical convergence expressed in multilateral and bilateral theological texts has greatly helped us to describe our common goal of the unity we seek.

17. In Chapter II we describe our common calling to full visible unity. We then proceed to record in ten points what we can now agree in faith (Chapter III). Consideration of the Ordained Ministry of the Church (Chapter IV) and of Apostolicity and Succession (Chapter V) follow. In Chapter VI we set out issues that still need to be faced by our two churches before we can take further steps towards the goal of visible unity. This Chapter also includes a brief description of how two churches of such different size might live in unity without losing their distinctive identities. The acknowledgements and commitments in the Declaration (Chapter VII) are framed on the basis of:

- the agreements in faith;
- our commitment to full, visible unity;
- our determination to resolve outstanding differences between us;
- and our firm commitment to intensify the relations between our two churches now.

18. While we hold full, visible unity as the desired long-term goal, at this time we propose that our churches declare their recognition of each other as churches belonging to the One, Holy, Catholic and Apostolic Church of Jesus Christ and we propose a series of steps which will draw us closer together, locally and nationally, under the guidance of the Holy Spirit.

---

[6] On 27 October 1982 Bishop Kenneth Woollcombe participated in the consecration of Bishop Geoffrey Birtill at the Fulneck Moravian Church, Pudsey, West Yorkshire. He did so in fulfilment of a promise made by Bishop David Brown of Guildford shortly before his death, and having ascertained that the Archbishop of York (Stuart Blanch) and the Bishop of Bradford (Geoffrey Paul) had no objections. Under Canon B 43.5 this is no longer possible.

II OUR COMMON CALLING TO FULL, VISIBLE UNITY

The Church as Sign, Instrument and Foretaste of the Kingdom of God

19. God's plan as declared in Holy Scripture is to reconcile all things in Christ, in, through and for whom they were made[7].

20. For this purpose God called Abraham, chose Israel, sent Jesus Christ and commissioned the Church for the blessing of all peoples. The servant of God will not only restore the scattered people of Israel; he is given 'as a light to the nations', to bring salvation to 'the end of the earth' (Is. 49. 6). In Christ God was reconciling the whole world to himself through the blood of the cross (2 Cor. 5. 19; Col. 1. 15-20), whereby our sins are forgiven (Eph. 1. 7). The Letter to the Ephesians recognizes the implications of the work of Christ for the mystery, the call and the mission of the Church, when it says 'God. . . has blessed us in Christ with every spiritual blessing. . . He has made known to us in all wisdom and insight the mystery of his will, according to his purpose which he set forth in Christ as a plan for the fulness of time, to unite all things in him, things in heaven and things on earth' (Eph. 1. 3, 9, 10). 'But grace was given to each of us according to the measure of Christ's gift . . . And his gifts were that some should be apostles, some prophets, some evangelists, some pastors and teachers, to equip the saints for the work of ministry, for building up the body of Christ, until we all attain to the unity of the faith and of the knowledge of the Son of God, to mature manhood, to the measure of the stature of the fulness of Christ' (Eph. 4. 7, 11-13).

21. The Church, the body of Christ, must always be seen in this perspective as instrumental to God's ultimate purpose. The Church exists for the glory of God and to serve, in obedience to the mission of Christ, the reconciliation of humankind and of all creation. Therefore the Church is sent into the world as a sign, instrument and foretaste of a reality which comes from beyond history – the Kingdom or Reign of God. It is already a

---

[7] Paras 19-23 are based on paras 1-5 of *The Meissen Common Statement (Meissen). The Meissen Agreement: Texts* (CCU Occasional Paper No. 2, 1992) contains the text of *The Meissen Common Statement,* together with the full text of the paragraphs cited in the footnotes.

provisional embodiment of God's will, which is the coming of the Kingdom.[8] The Church is a divine reality, holy and transcending present finite reality. At the same time, as a human institution, it shares in the sinfulness, the ambiguity and the frailty of the human condition, and is always in need of repentance, reform and renewal.[9]

The Church as Koinonia

22. Today we are re-discovering, together with other Christians, the character of the Church as communion. Underlying many of the New Testament descriptions of the Church, such as 'the people of God', 'the body of Christ', 'the bride', 'the temple of the Spirit', is the reality of a *koinonia* – a communion which is grounded in the life of the Holy Trinity, in which all the baptized share and in which all are joined to one another in that divine life.[10] This community – *koinonia* – is established by a baptism inseparable from faith and conversion. The vocation of all the baptized is to live as a corporate priesthood offering praise to God, sharing the good news and engaging in mission and service to humankind. This common life is sustained and nurtured by God's grace through word and sacrament. It is served by the ordained ministry and also held together by other bonds of communion.[11]

23. The Church is the community *(koinonia)* of those reconciled with God and with one another. It is the community of those who, in the power of the Holy Spirit, believe in Jesus Christ and are justified through God's grace. It is also the reconciling community because it has been called to bring to all humankind God's gracious offer of redemption and renewal.[12] Because the *koinonia* is also a participation in Christ crucified, it is also part of the nature and mission of the Church to share in the

---

[8] Cf. *God's Reign and Our Unity. The Report of the Anglican-Reformed International Commission 1981-1984.* Woking, England, January 1984 (London, 1984), paras 29f.

[9] Cf. *Anglican-Lutheran Dialogue. The Report of the Anglican-Lutheran European Regional Commission.* Helsinki, August-September 1982 (London, 1983) *(Helsinki)*, para. 47.

[10] The meaning of *koinonia* includes fellowship, participation, sharing, partaking, community, communion.

[11] Cf. para. 26 below.

[12] Cf. *Helsinki,* paras 49f, and Anglican-Roman Catholic International Commission, *The Final Report.* Windsor, September 1981 (London, 1982) (ARCIC I), Introduction, para. 8.

sufferings and struggles of humankind, in a world alienated from God and divided within itself by our disobedience to his will.

Steps towards Full, Visible Unity

24. The disunity of the Church impairs Christ's mission in the world.[13] It is within a missionary perspective that we can begin to overcome the divisions which have kept us apart. As our churches grow in faith into the fulness of Christ, so they will themselves grow together in unity. The unity we seek as members of the Church of England and the Moravian Church in Great Britain and Ireland is none other than that unity we seek with all Christians in the One, Holy, Catholic and Apostolic Church. This unity has been described in the statement *The Unity of The Church as Koinonia: Gift and Calling,* adopted by the Seventh Assembly of the World Council of Churches in Canberra in February 1991. This unity will reflect the different gifts God has given to his Church in many nations, languages, cultures and traditions. The unity we seek must at one and the same time respect these different gifts and manifest as fully as possible the oneness of the Church of Jesus Christ. 'In communion diversities are brought together in harmony as gifts of the Holy Spirit, contributing to the richness and fulness of the Church of God.'[14]

25. In God's Kingdom, all will be completely obedient to God and therefore totally reconciled to one another in God. But in a fallen world we are committed to strive for the 'full, visible unity' of the Body of Christ on earth. We are to work for the manifestation of unity at every level, a unity which is grounded in the life of the Holy Trinity and is God's purpose for the whole of creation. All our attempts to describe or realize this vision are bound to be provisional. We are continually being led to see fresh depths and riches of that unity and to grasp new ways in which it might be manifested in word and life. Every experience of unity is a gift of God and a foretaste and sign of the Kingdom.

26. As the churches grow together, the understanding of the characteristics of full, visible unity becomes clearer. We agree that full, visible unity must include:

---

[13] Paras 24-26 are based on *Meissen,* paras 6-8.

[14] The Canberra Statement is reproduced on pp. 85-7 below.

- *a common confession of the apostolic faith in word and life.* This one faith has to be confessed together, locally and universally, so that God's reconciling purpose is everywhere shown forth. Living this apostolic faith together, the Church helps the world to attain its proper destiny.

- *the sharing of one baptism, the celebrating of one eucharist and the service of a reconciled, common ministry.* This common participation in one baptism, one eucharist and one ministry unites 'all in each place' with 'all in every place' within the whole communion of saints. Every eucharist is the act of the risen and ascended Christ, in whom the whole Church, local and universal, is mysteriously present. Through visible unity the healing and uniting power of the Triune God is made evident amidst the divisions of humankind.

- *bonds of communion* which enable the Church at every level to guard and interpret the apostolic faith, to take decisions, to teach authoritatively, to share goods and to bear effective witness in the world. These bonds of communion will possess personal, collegial and communal aspects.[15] At every level they are outward and visible signs of the communion between persons who, through their baptism and eucharistic fellowship, are drawn into the fellowship of the Triune God.

27. This description of the characteristics of full, visible unity has been affirmed by the Church of England and the Evangelical Church in Germany in the Meissen Declaration. It bears close resemblance to the description of the visible unity of the Church set out in the Canberra Statement, which comes from the broadest ecumenical forum that exists. It says:

> The unity of the church to which we are called is a *koinonia* given and expressed in: the common confession of the apostolic faith; a common sacramental life entered by the one baptism and celebrated together in one eucharistic fellowship; a common life in which members and ministries are mutually recognized and reconciled; and a common mission witnessing to all people to the gospel of God's grace and serving the whole of creation. The goal of the

---

[15] Cf. para 28(j) below.

search for full communion is realized when all the churches are able to recognize in one another the one, holy, catholic and apostolic church in its fulness. This full communion will be expressed on the local and the universal levels through conciliar forms of life and action. In such communion churches are bound in all aspects of their faith together at all levels in confessing the one faith and engaging in worship and witness, deliberation and action.

III WHAT WE CAN NOW AGREE IN FAITH

28. In view of the substantial convergence in theological dialogue referred to earlier and the many insights affirmed in the Covenanting process, we can now record the following points of agreement:[16]

a   We accept the authority of and read the Scriptures of the Old and New Testaments. Each church provides a lectionary, and in the course of the Church's year appropriate Scriptures are read to mark the festivals and seasons.

b   We accept the Niceno-Constantinopolitan and Apostles' Creeds and confess the basic trinitarian and christological dogmas to which these creeds testify. That is, we believe that Jesus of Nazareth is true God and true Man, and that God is one God in three persons, Father, Son and Holy Spirit.[17]

c   We celebrate the apostolic faith in worship, and centrally in liturgical worship, which is both a celebration of salvation through Christ and a significant factor in forming the *consensus fidelium* (the common mind of the faithful). We rejoice at the extent of 'our common tradition of spirituality, liturgy and sacramental life', which has given us similar forms of worship, common texts, hymns, canticles and prayers. We are influenced by a common liturgical renewal. We also rejoice at the variety of expression shown in different cultural settings.[18]

d   Baptism is both God's gift and our human response to that gift in repentance and in faith.[19] It is a sign of God's gracious activity in the life of the person baptized. Baptism with water in the name of the Triune God is the sacrament of union with the death and resur-

---

[16]   This paragraph is based on *Meissen*, para. 15.

[17]   Cf. *Anglican Lutheran International Conversations: The Report of the Conversations 1970-1972, authorized by the Lambeth Conference and the Lutheran World Federation* (London, 1973) *(Pullach)*, paras 23-25.

[18]   Cf. *Helsinki*, para. 31; *Baptism, Eucharist and Ministry* (WCC Faith and Order Paper No.111, 1982) *(BEM), Baptism*, paras 17-23, *Eucharist*, paras 27-33, *Ministry*, paras 41-44.

[19]   Cf. BEM, *Baptism*, para. 8.

rection of Jesus Christ, initiating the one baptized into the One, Holy, Catholic and Apostolic Church. Baptism is related not only to a momentary experience, but to life-long growth into Christ.[20] Both our churches offer baptism to adults and infants and regard it as unrepeatable. Since we practise and value infant baptism, we also take seriously our catechetical task for the nurture of baptized children to mature commitment to Christ.[21] The life of the Christian is necessarily one of continuing struggle yet also of continuing experience of grace.[22] In both our traditions infant baptism is followed by a rite of confirmation, which includes invocation of the Triune God, renewal of the baptismal profession of faith and a prayer that through the renewal of the grace of baptism the candidate may be strengthened now and for ever.[23]

e   We believe that the celebration of the Eucharist (or the Lord's Supper or Holy Communion) is the feast of the new covenant instituted by Jesus Christ in which we set forth his life, death and resurrection and look for his coming in glory. In the Eucharist the risen Christ gives his body and blood under the visible signs of bread and wine to the Christian community. 'In the action of the Eucharist Christ is truly present to share his risen life with us and to unite us with himself in his self-offering to the Father, the one full, perfect and sufficient sacrifice which he alone can offer and has offered once for all.'[24] In the Eucharist, through the power of the Holy Spirit, the Church experiences the love of God and the forgiveness of sins in Jesus Christ and proclaims his death and resurrection until he comes and brings his Kingdom to completion.[25]

f   We believe and proclaim the gospel, that in his great love God, through Christ, redeems the world. We 'share a common under-

---

[20]   BEM, Baptism, para. 9.

[21]   Conversations between the British and Irish Anglican Churches and the Nordic and Baltic Lutheran Churches, *The Porvoo Common Statement* (CCU Occasional Paper No. 3, 1993) *(Porvoo)*, para. 32(g).

[22]   BEM, Baptism, para. 9.

[23]   Cf. *Porvoo*, para. 32(g).

[24]   *God's Reign and Our Unity*, para. 65.

[25]   Cf. *BEM, Eucharist*, para. 1.

standing of God's justifying grace, i.e. that we are accounted righteous and are made righteous before God only by grace through faith because of the merits of our Lord and Saviour Jesus Christ, and not on account of our works or merits . . . Both our traditions affirm that justification leads and must lead to "good works"; authentic faith issues in love'.[26]

g We share a common hope in the final consummation of the Kingdom of God, and believe that in this eschatological perspective we are called to work now for the furtherance of justice and peace. Our life in the world and in the Church is governed by the obligations of the Kingdom. 'The Christian faith is that God has made peace through Jesus "by the blood of his cross" (Col. 1. 20), so establishing the one valid centre for the unity of the whole human family.'[27]

h We believe that the Church is constituted and sustained by the Triune God through God's saving action in word and sacraments, and is not the creation of individual believers. We believe that the Church is sent into the world as sign, instrument and foretaste of the Kingdom of God. But we also recognize that the Church, being at the same time a human organization, stands in constant need of reform and renewal.[28]

i We believe that all members of the Church are called to participate in its apostolic mission. There are therefore various gifts of the Holy Spirit for the building up of the community and the fulfilment of its calling.[29] Within the community of the Church the ordained ministry exists to serve the ministry of the whole people of God. We hold the ordained ministry of word and sacrament to be a gift of God to his Church and therefore an office of divine institution.[30]

Both our churches have a threefold ministry of bishop, presbyter and deacon and believe it to serve as an expression of the unity we

---

[26] *Helsinki*, para. 20; cf. paras 17-21.

[27] *God's Reign and Our Unity*, para. 18; cf. para. 43 and *Pullach*, para. 59.

[28] Cf. para. 21 above.

[29] Cf. *BEM, Ministry*, para. 7.

[30] Cf. *Helsinki*, paras 32-43, *God's Reign and Our Unity*, paras 91-97, *BEM, Ministry*, paras 4 and 12.

seek and also a means of achieving it.[31] Within this threefold ministry the bishop signifies and focuses the continuity and unity of the whole Church. Apostolic continuity and unity in both our churches is expressed in the consecration and ordination of bishops in succession. The ordination of other ministers in both our churches is always by a bishop, with the assent of the community of the Church.[32] Integrally linked with episcopal ordination is our common tradition that the bishop has a special pastoral care for the clergy as for the whole Church.

j   A ministry of oversight *(episcope)* is a gift of God to the Church. In both our Churches it is exercised in personal, collegial and communal ways. It is necessary in order to witness to and safeguard the unity and apostolicity of the Church.[33] In both our traditions in the course of history the exact structure and distribution of oversight functions have varied.

---

[31]   Cf. *BEM, Ministry*, para. 22.

[32]   Cf. 'The Office of Bishop in our Churches: Texts', appended to this Common Statement.

[33]   Cf. *BEM, Ministry*, paras 23 and 26, *Pullach*, para. 79; *God's Reign and Our Unity*, para. 92.

IV THE ORDAINED MINISTRY OF THE CHURCH

29. Jesus Christ is the unique priest of the new covenant. Christ's life was given as a sacrifice for all. Derivatively, the Church as a whole can be described as a priesthood. All members are called to offer their being 'as a living sacrifice' and to intercede for the Church and the salvation of the world.[34] Within the priesthood of the whole Church, the ministry of the ordained is an appointed means through which Christ makes his priesthood present and effective to his people. The ordained ministry has a representative function, both in relation to Christ and in relation to the community of faith, and the ordained fulfil a particular priestly service by strengthening and building up the royal and prophetic priesthood of the faithful through word and sacraments, through their prayers of intercession, and through their pastoral guidance of the community.[35]

30. The New Testament does not describe a single pattern of ministry which might serve as a blueprint or continuing norm for all future ministry. Nevertheless a threefold pattern of bishops, presbyters (priests) and deacons became the established pattern in the early Church and has been retained by many churches including our two churches.[36] However, the distribution of functions between the three orders has varied, and still varies today.

31. Both our Churches find the statements concerning the threefold ministry in *Baptism, Eucharist and Ministry* consonant with their own understanding. We believe that the threefold ministry of deacon, presbyter and bishop may serve today as a means of expressing unity. At the same time we recognize that in other churches different forms of the ordained ministry have been blessed with the gifts of the Holy Spirit. We believe there is a single ordained ministry which takes a threefold form. In both our churches, only ordained persons are authorized to preside at

---

[34] *BEM, Ministry*, para. 17.

[35] Cf. *BEM, Ministry*, para. 17 and commentary.

[36] Cf. *BEM, Ministry*, para 19. In the early Church the terms 'priesthood' and 'priest' came to be used to designate the ordained ministry and minister as presiding at the eucharist (*BEM, Ministry*, para. 17: commentary).

the eucharist. In both our churches the significance of the order of deacon as a servant ministry is maintained in the diaconal quality of the presbyterate and episcopate.

32. As stated in *Baptism, Eucharist and Ministry, deacons* represent to the Church its calling as servant in the world. By struggling in Christ's name with the myriad needs of societies and persons, deacons exemplify the interdependence of worship and service in the Church's life. They exercise responsibility in the worship of the congregation: for example by reading the scriptures, preaching and leading the people in prayer. They help in the teaching of the congregation. They exercise a ministry of love within the community. They fulfil certain administrative tasks and may be elected to responsibilities for governance.[37]

33. *Presbyters* serve as pastoral ministers of word and sacraments in a local eucharistic community. They are preachers and teachers of the faith, exercise pastoral care and bear responsibility for the discipline of the congregation, to the end that the world may believe and that the entire membership of the Church may be renewed, strengthened and equipped in ministry.[38]

34. *Bishops* guard the faith, preach the word, preside at the sacraments and ordain. Bishops meet collegially and in synods with clergy and laity, and are representative ministers of continuity and unity in the Church. Bishops have a pastoral role and are pastors of the pastors. Bishops have a special responsibility for mission. They have a role in relating the local Christian community to the wider Church, and the universal Church to their community. They, in communion with the presbyters and deacons and the whole community, are responsible for the orderly continuation of ministerial authority in the Church.[39]

Questions about Ministry to be Faced Together

35. The traditional threefold pattern to which we are committed raises questions for both our churches. We need to face together how the threefold ministry can be fully developed for the most effective witness of the Church in today's world.

---

[37] BEM, *Ministry*, para. 31.
[38] BEM, *Ministry*, para. 30.
[39] Cf. BEM, *Ministry*, para. 29.

36. The diaconate has become, in most cases, a probationary ministry leading to the presbyterate, leaving our churches without much experience of diaconal ministry within the threefold order. The Diocese of Portsmouth, however, has had a permanent diaconate for several years. This, together with the ordination of women to the diaconate in the Church of England and their experience of this role, has made a valuable contribution to the Church's understanding of the order of deacon. In the Moravian Church the probationary status of the diaconate includes authorization to preside at the eucharist and confirmation. Any re-examination of the diaconate should affirm that it is a distinctive order, to be valued alongside the presbyterate and the episcopate.

37. In the Church of England, confirmation is invariably administered by the bishop. In the Moravian Church, it is administered by the local minister. Both of these practices have precedents in earlier centuries and both are currently accepted in other episcopal churches. The theology and practice of confirmation is under discussion in a number of churches.

38. Both our churches exercise oversight *(episcope)* in personal, collegial and communal forms. However the precise relation between these forms of oversight is not always clear. In the Church of England, for example, the relation of the collegiality of the House of Bishops to the General Synod is a matter of debate.

39. The expression of episcopacy in both the international *Unitas Fratrum* and the Anglican Communion is shaped by ecumenical relationships as well as the surrounding culture. The most obvious difference in the expression of episcopacy between our two churches is that in the Church of England the bishop has both pastoral and juridical functions and, whether diocesan or suffragan, relates to a diocesan area. In the Moravian Church the bishop's function is primarily pastoral, and he relates to the province in which he resides, but not necessarily to a specific area within it. Juridical authority in the Moravian Church lies with the Provincial Board.

40. The Church of England is growing in its awareness of the importance of the collegiality of the bishops.[40] In the synodical government of the

---

[40] Cf. *Episcopal Ministry. The Report of the Archbishops' Group on the Episcopate* (GS 944, London, 1990), chapter 11.

Church of England the House of Bishops has a special responsibility for guiding the Church on matters of faith and order. At the international level, such collegiality is expressed in the Anglican Communion in the Lambeth Conference. The first international Moravian bishops' conference in recent times, held in 1992, reflected a similar growth in awareness of the importance of collegiality, and it is proposed that in future such a bishops' conference, and also regional meetings of bishops, should be held regularly.

V APOSTOLICITY AND SUCCESSION

41. We believe in a Church which is apostolic. 'As thou hast sent me into the world, so I have sent them' (John 17. 18). The whole Church, and every member of it, is called by Christ to participate in, and contribute to, the communication of the gospel by a faithful expression and embodiment in a given time and place of the permanent characteristics of the Church of the apostles. Apostolic tradition in the Church means continuity in the permanent characteristics of the Church of the apostles.[41] Within the apostolicity of the whole Church is an apostolic succession of the ordained ministry which serves and gives focus to the continuity of the Church in its life in Christ and in its faithfulness to the words and acts of Jesus transmitted by the apostles.[42]

42. The continuity of the ordained ministry is to be understood within the continuity of the apostolic life and mission of the whole Church. Apostolic succession in the episcopal office is a visible and personal way of focusing the apostolicity of the whole Church.[43]

43. The continuity of the Church in apostolic succession is signified in the consecration or ordination of a bishop. In episcopal consecration the laying on of hands with prayer by the ordaining bishops (themselves so consecrated) bears witness to God's faithfulness to his people and to the promised presence of Christ with his Church to the end of time; secondly, it expresses the Church's intention to be faithful to God's initiative and gift, by living in the continuity of the apostolic faith and tradition; thirdly, the participation of a group of bishops in the laying on of hands signifies their churches' acceptance of the new bishop. This expresses the catholicity of the Church. Thus in the act of consecration a bishop receives in faith the sign of divine approval and the commission to lead his particular church in the common faith and apostolic life of all the churches.[44]

---

[41] *BEM, Ministry*, para. 34.

[42] Cf. *Porvoo*, para. 40, *BEM, Ministry*, para. 34: commentary.

[43] Cf. *Porvoo*, para 46.

[44] Cf. *Porvoo*, paras 47-49.

44. We believe that to ordain in historic succession is a sign that the Church intends to remain faithful to its apostolic teaching and mission. Neither the sign of ordination nor the sign of an unbroken ministerial succession guarantees the fidelity of any particular church to every aspect of apostolic faith and life; nor does it guarantee the personal faithfulness of those ordained in this way. Nonetheless we believe that to ordain in historic succession is an effective sign of continuity with the characteristics of the Church of the apostles.[45]

45. Both our churches have been characterized by an intention to be true to the faith and order of the primitive or apostolic Church. Both churches have considered it essential that ministry should be in continuity with that of the apostles. Both have carefully maintained a personal episcopal succession, in which bishops are consecrated with the laying on of hands by bishops themselves so consecrated.

46. In the past, both our churches have sought to recover the purity of the primitive Church. The formation of the *Unitas Fratrum* in the mid-fifteenth century reflected such a desire. Its founders rejected the charge that in ordaining ministers for their church in 1467 they had devised something new. They believed they were being faithful to the primitive Church and the teaching of the apostles. Their desire to live in continuity with the Church of the apostles was demonstrated when they obtained ordination from the Waldensians, whom they saw as representing a pure succession of apostolic teaching and apostolic life from the primitive Church.[46] A similar concern marked the Reformation in England. The Reformers sought, by removing later accretions, to recover the pure faith and order of the primitive Church.

47. In England this recovery could be achieved without a break in the continuity of structures and episcopal succession with the existing English Church. In 1559 bishops could be found who were willing to consecrate Matthew Parker, and when the Interregnum ended in 1660 there were still a few Church of England bishops alive to consecrate new bishops. Thus the Church of England has been able to maintain an unbroken succession of episcopal consecrations. For the *Unitas Fratrum* in the mid-

---

[45] Cf. *Porvoo*, paras 50-51.

[46] See the essay 'The Origins of our Churches: The Bohemian Brethren' appended to this Common Statement.

sixteenth century circumstances were otherwise; in 1553, when the only bishop was in prison and believed dead, two new bishops were consecrated by presbyters. However, the Moravian Church has inherited and continued an episcopal succession unbroken since 1553.[47] The guarding and handing on of this succession from the 1620s, when the *Unitas Fratrum* was all but extinguished in Bohemia and Moravia, until 1735, when Daniel Ernst Jablonski, one of the old *Unitas Fratrum*'s last bishops, was able to consecrate David Nitschmann as the first bishop of the renewed Moravian Church, demonstrates the importance which the *Unitas Fratrum* has attached to the continuance of an episcopal ministry in ordered succession.

48. In spite of our different histories, what remains important for both our churches is our intention to continue the ministry of the Church of the apostles in faithfulness to its mission, teaching and life. Our experience and history lead us to believe that the full, visible unity of the Church will be served by an episcopal ministry in a succession of bishops consecrated with prayer and the laying on of hands of those so consecrated and in continuity with the ministry of the universal Church. The firm intention of our churches for the future, as it has been in the past, is to continue an episcopal succession so ordered.

---

[47] *ibid.*

VI ISSUES STILL TO BE FACED

49. In our Conversations we have achieved a significant theological convergence. We have come to the point when we can acknowledge each other as churches with authentic ministries and sacraments. We have identifed many ways in which our churches could commit themselves now to grow together, which would not entail legal changes.

50. We have also glimpsed a vision of visible unity which would not involve a loss of identity of either partner. We consider it important to give some account, as far as we can, of the shape that visible unity between our churches might take in England. That unity would entail a common confession of the apostolic faith in word and in life; the sharing of one baptism, the celebrating of one eucharist and the service of a reconciled, interchangeable, common ministry in historic succession; bonds of communion to guard and interpret the apostolic faith, to take decisions, to teach authoritatively, to share goods and to bear effective witness in the world. We also believe that visible unity between our two churches in this country would inevitably carry implications for our world communions and would be a significant step on the way to the unity of all Anglicans and Moravians.

51. It is important that the distinctive 'ethos' of both traditions should be nurtured and shared within visible unity, including:

- spirituality
- liturgy
- hymnody
- ways of doing theology
- ways of being a Christian community
- styles of oversight and episcopacy
- styles of mission
- ways of honouring the memory of our histories
- commemoration of our saints and martyrs and memorial days

- links with the Moravian Unity and the Anglican Communion
- the honouring of other ecumenical partnerships.

52. We believe that the development of such a model of common life would be a significant contribution towards the discovery of a unity which encourages and safeguards diversity – a communion with diversity. This could provide a model for a more inclusive united Church in England and give assurance to those who fear that commitment to visible unity might lead towards a monolithic organizational structure. Indeed the unity we seek with others will not be less diverse than the comprehensiveness that is already found in our churches.

53. There are, however, several issues upon which further convergence would be required before that visible unity with diversity could be achieved:

- a re-appraisal of the three orders of ministry (in particular the diaconate) in the light of the emerging ecumenical consensus and the insights of our traditions – we are encouraged that fresh thinking on the diaconate is already emerging in both churches;
- the role of the episcopate within a 'united' church to express the unity of the whole Church while at the same time to safeguard the distinctive identity of the traditions;
- the process of formally reconciling our two ministries;
- the exercise of authority;
- how within a united church the particular gifts and distinctive ethos of both traditions could be sustained and enrich each other;

These are separate but inter-related matters.

54. We list these issues on which we need further agreement within a firm intention to work towards their resolution. The closer relation between our churches established on the basis of this Common Statement will provide a secure context for facing outstanding issues. Above all, we believe that it is only by continuous conversion to Christ that we shall come nearer to one another in Christ: and by continuous re-formation of our lives that we shall grow nearer to one another and become renewed and enriched in a common life.

VII OUR COMMON FUTURE

55. On the basis of:

- the agreement we have expressed in the foregoing chapters;
- our determination to resolve outstanding differences between us;
- our commitment to intensify the relations between our two churches as a step on the way to the goal of full visible unity;

we recommend that our churches jointly make the following declaration:

THE FETTER LANE DECLARATION

We, the Church of England and the Moravian Church in Great Britain and Ireland, in the light of what we have re-discovered of our common history and heritage and on the basis of our common understanding of our calling to full, visible unity (Chapter II), our fundamental agreement in faith (Chapter III), our understanding of the ordained ministry of the Church (Chapter IV), and our agreement on apostolicity and succession (Chapter V), make the following acknowledgements and commitments.

a.

   (i) We acknowledge one another's churches as churches belonging to the One, Holy, Catholic and Apostolic Church of Jesus Christ and truly participating in the apostolic mission of the whole people of God;

   (ii) We acknowledge that in our churches the Word of God is authentically preached and the sacraments of baptism and eucharist are duly administered;[*]

---

[*] Cf. Article XIX of the Thirty-nine Articles of the Church of England: 'The visible Church of Christ is a congregation of faithful men, in the which the pure Word of God is preached, and the Sacraments be duly ministered according to Christ's ordinance in all those things that of necessity are requisite to the same'.

(iii) We acknowledge that both our churches share in the common confession of the apostolic faith;

(iv) We acknowledge the extent of our common traditions of spirituality and liturgy, which have given us similar forms of worship, common texts, hymns, canticles and prayers;

(v) We acknowledge one another's ordained ministries, ordered in a threefold pattern, as given by God and as instruments of his grace by which our churches are served and built up, and look forward to the time when our churches are united and our ministries are interchangeable;

(vi) We acknowledge in our churches an episcopal ministry through which both churches intend to continue the ministry of the universal Church and to maintain and signify the apostolicity and catholicity of the Church. This intention has been signified in the laying on of hands by those already so consecrated.

(vii) We acknowledge that personal and collegial oversight *(episkope)* is embodied and exercised in our churches in a variety of forms, episcopal and synodical, as a visible sign of the Church's unity and continuity in apostolic life, mission and ministry.

b. We commit ourselves to share a common life and mission. We will take all possible steps to visible unity in as many areas of life and witness as possible.

As the next steps towards that goal we agree:*

(i) to worship together and to pray for and with one another;

(ii) on the basis of our common baptism to welcome one another's baptized members to receive sacramental and other pastoral ministrations:

(iii) to encourage the invitation of authorized ministers of our churches to minister in the other church in accordance with existing regulations (cf. Canon B 43 of the Church of England);

---

* It should be noted that some of these steps are already occurring in certain places.

(iv) taking into account other ecumenical partnerships and formal relations to encourage the establishment of Local Ecumenical Partnerships (LEPs) wherever a Moravian and an Anglican congregation live in the same community (cf. Canon B 44 of the Church of England);

(v) to participate as observers by invitation in each other's forms of oversight, including meetings of bishops and synods;

(vi) to train candidates for ordained and lay ministries of our churches together where appropriate;

(vii) to share our resources appropriately in order to strengthen the mission of the Church;

(viii) to help our own members and members of other churches to appreciate and draw out the distinctive gifts which each of our traditions has to offer to the wider Church;

(ix) to share the insight of our Common Statement with Anglicans and Moravians in other parts of the world, and to invite our international bodies to consider the implications of this Agreement for their consultative processes.

(c) In order to promote these steps, we commit ourselves to establish a contact group of lay and ordained persons to oversee the implementation of those things which are already possible, to ensure that further consideration is given to those areas where convergence is still required and to nurture our growth in communion.

56. We recommend to our churches that this agreement and the new relationship established by it be inaugurated and affirmed in a celebration which reflects its national and local dimensions.

PARTICIPANTS IN THE CONVERSATIONS

Representatives of the Moravian Church in Great Britain and Ireland

The Rt Revd Geoffrey Birtill, Bishop of the *Unitas Fratrum* (Chairman)
The Revd Richard Connor
The Revd Fred Linyard
The Revd David Newman (from May 1991)
The Revd John Smith

Representatives of the Church of England

The Rt Revd Peter Coleman, Bishop of Crediton (Chairman)
The Revd Canon Peter Boulton (until February 1994)
The Revd William Croft (from October 1991)
The Revd Dr Margaret Guite (until February 1992)
The Very Revd Robert Jeffery, Dean of Worcester (from October 1991)

Consultant

The Revd Prebendary Dr Paul Avis (from November 1994)

Staff

Dr Mary Tanner
Dr Colin Podmore
The Revd Donald Reece (from November 1994)

All papers were sent to the Archbishop of Canterbury's Assistant Secretary for Ecumenical Affairs, and copies of the minutes were sent to representatives of the Church of Ireland.

Essays in Moravian and Anglican History

by Colin Podmore

CONTENTS

	Page
The Origins and Development of our Churches	37
The Church of England	37
The Church of the Bohemian Brethren	45
The Moravian Church	63
The *Unitas Fratrum* and the Church of England	72

Note

These essays were written at the request of the Conversations. Parts of the third and fourth essays are based on doctoral research which I undertook before joining the staff of the General Synod in 1988. I am indebted to members of the Conversations, the Faith and Order Advisory Group and the Council for Christian Unity for suggestions which led to improvements to the text, but the responsibility for judgements made and opinions expressed remains my own.

Colin Podmore   December 1995

THE ORIGINS AND DEVELOPMENT OF OUR CHURCHES

THE CHURCH OF ENGLAND

When Christianity came to Britain is not known, although some evidence suggests a Christian presence by about 200. In 314 the Church was sufficiently well established to be represented by the Bishops of London, York and a third British see at the Council of Arles. In the fifth century, however, Southern and Eastern Britain was invaded by pagan Angles, Saxons and Jutes. The Church continued in Wales, and in the sixth century Cornwall was evangelized from there and from Ireland. It was from Ireland, too, that St Columba (c.521-597) travelled to found Iona, from whence St Aidan (d. 651) led the mission which was to re-establish the Church in Northumbria. He was consecrated bishop in 635 and established his see on Lindisfarne. Meanwhile, in 597, St Augustine (d. c.604) had landed in Kent at the head of a mission sent by the Pope, St Gregory the Great, to re-evangelize England.[1]

Although St Augustine's mission was thus by no means the only source of English Christianity, the *Ecclesia Anglicana* (Anglican or English Church) can be said to stem chiefly from it. Seventy years after Augustine's arrival, however, the English Church was in a state of some disorder. Theodore of Tarsus (c.602-690) was sent from Rome to become Archbishop of Canterbury, arriving in 669. Having supplied bishops for the many vacant sees, he called a council which met at Hertford in 672. This council involved the whole English Church, and agreed a set of canons which could be described as its founding charter.[2] Bede described Theodore as 'the first of the archbishops whom the whole English Church consented to obey'. Perhaps Theodore's most lasting achievement was the creation

---

[1] For a recent survey of the history of episcopacy in the Church of England, see C. Hill, 'Episcopacy in our Churches: England' in *Together in Mission and Ministry. The Porvoo Common Statement with Essays on Church and Ministry in Northern Europe* (GS 1083, London, 1993), pp.125-136.

[2] P. Wormald, 'The Venerable Bede and the "Church of the English"' in D.G. Rowell (ed.), *The English Religious Tradition and the Genius of Anglicanism* (Wantage, 1992), p.17.

of the English diocesan system. Dividing the existing large dioceses, most of which covered the area of one of the English kingdoms, he established diocesan boundaries which are still recognizable today. It is not too much to claim that Theodore was the English Church's second founder.

The division of the English Church into two provinces dates from 735, when Pope Gregory III approved the raising of the bishopric of York to an archbishopric. Lanfranc (c.1042-1089), who was Archbishop of Canterbury from 1070, asserted the supremacy of Canterbury over York, but this was not finally settled until 1353, when it was accepted that the Archbishop of Canterbury should be styled Primate of All England and the Archbishop of York Primate of England. By the beginning of the fifteenth century the Convocations of Canterbury and York, provincial synods each consisting of an upper house of bishops and a lower house of clergy, had taken shape.

The English Reformation

The series of events which are collectively described as 'the English Reformation' took place over thirty years, in several distinct phases, beginning with the meeting of the Reformation Parliament in 1529 and culminating in the 'Elizabethan Settlement' of 1559. What may (anachronistically) be termed 'Anglicanism', as a distinctive body of beliefs, was, however, to reach maturity only in the following century.

The first phase, under Henry VIII, was essentially political. On 15 May 1532 the Convocation of Canterbury agreed the Submission of the Clergy, whereby the Convocations could only meet if summoned by royal writ and could make no canons without royal licence. Canon law was subordinated to the common and statute law of England. Acts of Parliament abolished payments and appeals from England to Rome, and the Pope's legal rights in England were divided between the Crown and the Archbishops. The 1534 Act of Supremacy declared that the King was 'the only supreme head in earth of the Church of England'. Between 1536 and 1540 the monastic houses of England were dissolved, a development which arguably owed more to the Crown's need for money and the financial aspirations of its supporters than to any strictly theological or ecclesiastical motives. Thus, in the reign of Henry VIII the English

Church was effectively separated and nationalized. The King replaced the Pope and seized a considerable proportion of the Church's wealth, but with the notable exception of the monastic life, its internal system remained intact. An English Bible was ordered to be placed in every parish church (1538) and an English Litany introduced (1544), but otherwise little official doctrinal or liturgical change occurred. Henry VIII died in 1547, over seventeen years after the meeting of the Reformation Parliament, never having heard the Mass other than in Latin.

The second phase of the English Reformation occurred in the brief but turbulent reign of Edward VI (1547-1553). Now there was doctrinal change, but, significantly, it was expressed first and foremost in liturgical change, centrally in the Prayer Books of 1549 and 1552, of which the Archbishop of Canterbury, Thomas Cranmer, was the chief author. The Church of England would continue to express its beliefs chiefly in its liturgy. Cranmer's liturgies built on the medieval liturgical tradition, echoing its prayers. In this they resembled those of German Lutheranism, another important influence, and differed from the essentially non-liturgical worship of the Swiss Reformed churches. Doctrinally, however, the 1552 Prayer Book showed Reformed influence, as did the Forty-two Articles which followed in 1553. One important difference was that the English Ordinal consciously retained the term 'priest' and provided for the continuation of the three orders of bishop, priest and deacon inherited from the early Church. In this second phase of the Reformation, liturgy and doctrine had been changed, but again the historic structure and order of the Church remained intact.

In the even briefer reign of Mary (1553-1558), most of the changes of her father and brother were undone. Reginald Pole, as papal legate, was invited to reconcile England to the Holy See, and on 30 November 1555 500 members of Parliament knelt to receive his absolution, as did the Convocation of Canterbury six days later. The Papal Supremacy and the Latin Mass were restored. In 1556 Cardinal Pole succeeded Cranmer as Archbishop of Canterbury, but he was to be the last archbishop who was in communion with the See of Rome. He and his Queen both died on 17 November 1558.

By the 1559 Act of Supremacy Elizabeth I accepted the amended title 'Supreme Governor of the Church of England'. The 1559 Act of

Uniformity re-introduced the 1552 Book of Common Prayer, slightly amended in a conservative direction. Of the bishops, only those of Llandaff and Sodor and Man remained in office. Matthew Parker was appointed Archbishop of Canterbury and consecrated in Lambeth Palace Chapel on 17 December 1559. None of Mary's bishops being willing to act, the consecration was performed by three former diocesan bishops and a suffragan. Again, liturgy preceded doctrinal definition. In 1562-3 the Forty-two Articles were amended and reduced in number, and as the Thirty-nine Articles they reached their final form in 1570. The Articles can be characterized as moderately Reformed, but were so framed as to comprehend as many as possible within the Church of England. The 1604 Canons of the Church of England furnished the Church with a code of canon law, but did not repeal the mediaeval canon law in areas which they did not address.

The English Reformation was marked not by innovation but by rejection of the innovations of Rome. Its intention was to get back to the pure faith and order of the early or 'primitive' Church. This position was defended against Roman Catholic criticism on the one hand by Bishop John Jewel (1522-71) in his *Apology* (1562) and against Puritan insistence that the Church of England was not fully reformed by Richard Hooker (c.1554-1600). In the seventeenth century this concern led to a flowering of patristic scholarship on the part of Anglican divines which was unrivalled in any other church, and devotion to the ideal of the primitive Church was to persist into the middle years of the eighteenth century and beyond.[3]

Abolition and Restoration

First, however, this developing Anglican tradition was driven underground or into exile by the victory of Parliament over Charles I in the Civil War (1642-1646). In 1645 Archbishop William Laud and then in 1649 the King himself were executed. During this radical break in the Church of England's history, its structure, episcopal ministry and liturgy were abolished. Only its buildings remained, and they were despoiled. From as early

---

[3] See E. Duffy, 'Primitive Christianity Revived; Religious Renewal in Augustan England', *Studies in Church History*, xiv (1977), 287-300.

as 1651 concern grew amongst loyal churchmen that the Church of England's episcopal succession might die out, and indeed by the end of 1659 all but nine of its 27 sees were vacant. The exiled King Charles II repeatedly attempted to persuade the survivors to consecrate new bishops, but they were too fearful to act on his orders within England, while age and infirmity held them back from travelling to the Continent. Had the Interregnum lasted even just ten years longer, the Anglican episcopal succession would probably have been extinguished.

In fact, after the Restoration of the Monarchy in 1660, the episcopally-ordered Church of England was restored also. Under the 1662 Act of Uniformity, some 1,900 clergy who were not episcopally ordained or who refused to use the revised Book of Common Prayer were ejected. After the 'Glorious Revolution' (1689) toleration was preferred to comprehension, and it was tacitly accepted that there would continue to be substantial bodies of Christians who dissented from the Church of England and maintained a separate religious life. The Church of England was now settled in its identity. In the eighteenth century, the Church of England's failure to retain John Wesley's Methodism within its structures increased the proportion of English Christians who did not belong to it, as did large-scale (Roman Catholic) Irish immigration in the following century.

The Nineteenth and Twentieth Centuries

During the nineteenth century a number of developments and movements greatly affected the Church of England's character. From the 1830s, ecclesiastical reforms began to modernize the Church's organization and redistribute its revenues, while Evangelicals, Liberals and Catholics occupied increasingly distinctive positions. Each of these streams has its successors today, and in addition to this, practices and insights which were originally distinctive to each of them can now be found much more widely within the Church of England. Visually (in the conduct of worship, liturgical dress, church furnishings, etc.) and in terms of its understanding of its own identity, the image which the Church of England overall has presented in the second half of the twentieth century owes more to the anglo-catholic Oxford Movement and its successors than to either of the other streams. In these respects, the Church of England as a whole would have been very different had it not been for the

Oxford Movement. *The Tracts for the Times* (1833-41), whose main authors were John Henry Newman, John Keble and Edward Bouverie Pusey, stressed the Church of England's identity as part of the Catholic Church and the apostolic authority of its bishops, derived from the historic, apostolic succession. Significantly, one of the Tractarians' chief projects was the 83-volume *Library of Anglo-Catholic Theology* (1841-1863), an edition of the works of the most notable seventeenth-century Anglican divines. This was the heritage which the Tractarians revived and on which they built, and its influence can be seen in the fact that the other great Tractarian publishing project was a *Library of the Fathers* (translations of the major patristic writings). As time went on, the Oxford Movement's emphasis on sacramental worship combined with other Victorian influences to revive catholic ritual, architecture and church furnishing and enrich the Church of England's worship liturgically and musically. It also resulted in the revival of religious orders in the Church of England.

The twentieth century has seen a gradual increase in the practical independence of the Church from the State. In 1919 the Church Assembly, consisting of the Convocations and a House of Laity, was established to process church legislation, which Parliament would approve or reject but not amend. In 1970 a new General Synod, inheriting most of the powers of the Convocations (which continued to exist) and all those of the Church Assembly, was inaugurated. By the Worship and Doctrine Measure 1974 the General Synod received powers to authorize new and alternative services without Parliamentary approval. Under a protocol of 1977, a church body, the Crown Appointments Commission, was given a decisive role in the appointment of diocesan bishops. A new code of canon law was promulged by the Convocations between 1964 and 1969, replacing the Canons of 1604, and in the Alternative Service Book (1980) the Church gained a definitive modern liturgy to complement the historic liturgy of the Book of Common Prayer.

In February 1994 the General Synod promulged a canon providing for the ordination of women to the priesthood. This was seen by the majority as a legitimate development of the ordained ministry, but by a substantial minority as effecting a major change in the Church of England's identity and self-understanding as part of the Catholic Church. Provision was made by Act of Synod for the continuing diversity of opinion in the Church of England in this matter.

The Church of England's understanding of its identity today is set out in the Preface to the Declaration of Assent:

> The Church of England is part of the one, holy, catholic, and apostolic Church, worshipping the one true God, Father, Son and Holy Spirit. It professes the faith uniquely revealed in the holy Scriptures and set forth in the catholic creeds, which faith the Church is called upon to proclaim afresh in each generation. Led by the Holy Spirit, it has borne witness to Christian truth in its historic formularies, the Thirty-nine Articles of Religion, the Book of Common Prayer and the Ordering of Bishops, Priests, and Deacons . . .

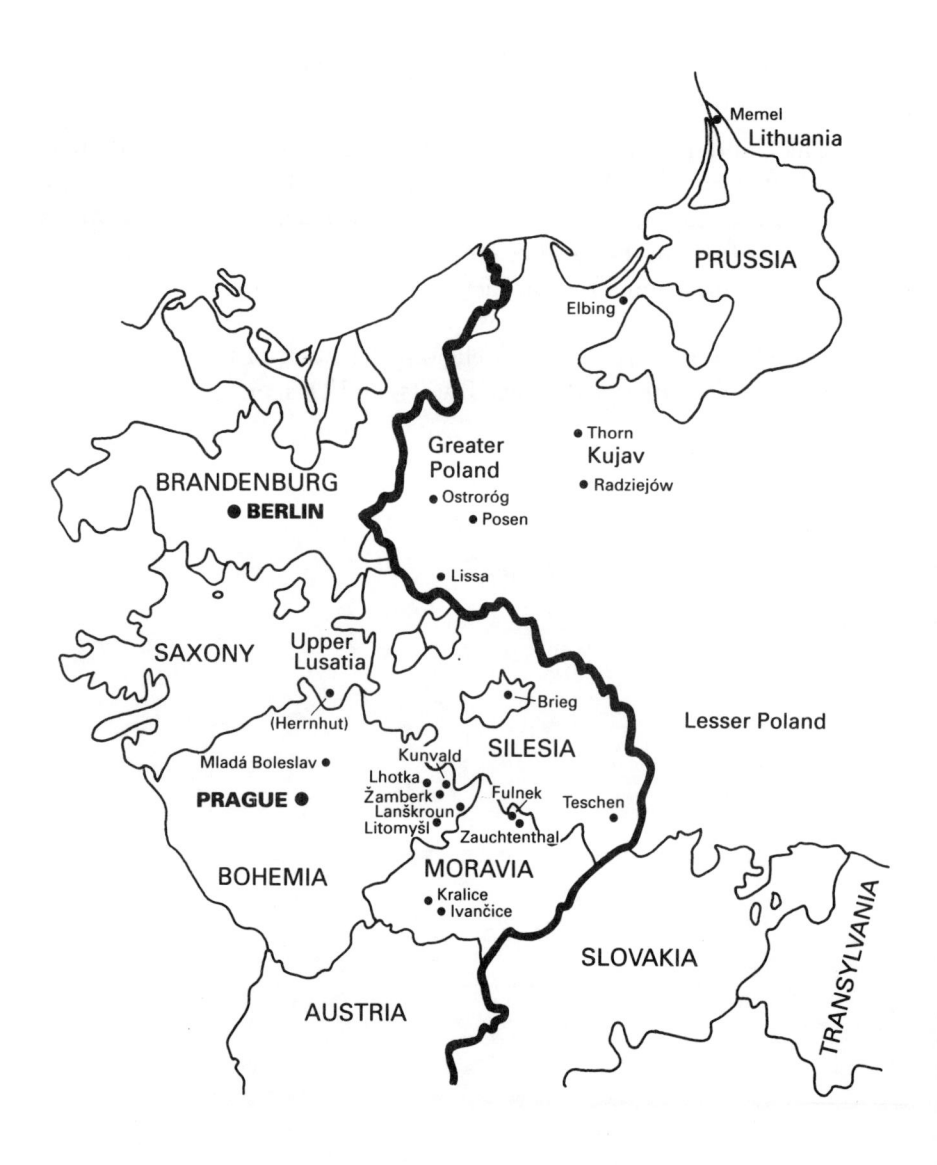

BOHEMIA, MORAVIA AND POLAND IN 1660

Only places mentioned in the text are shown (n.b. Herrnhut was founded in 1722). The thick line indicates the border of the Empire.

Territories under Habsburg rule included Austria, Bohemia, Moravia, Silesia and Slovakia. Brandenburg and Prussia were united under Hohenzollern rule.

THE CHURCH OF THE BOHEMIAN BRETHREN

The ultimate roots of the Church of the Bohemian Brethren lay in the church reform movement which grew up in Bohemia in the later fourteenth century.[1] Among the influences on the Czech reformers were the English reformer John Wyclif (c.1330-1384) and his 'Lollard' followers, and the Waldensians, a movement initiated in Lyons in the 1170s by Peter Valdes which was represented in German communities in Southern Bohemia. The Lollards and the Waldensians had a number of concerns in common, and indeed may be seen as aspects of a single movement. They questioned clerical dominance, pointed to clerical corruption, and pressed for lay access to the Scriptures and a more active role for the laity in the life and work of the Church.

Academic and popular streams in the Bohemian reform movement were united in the person of Jan Hus (c.1372-1415), a university teacher who also preached in Prague's reformist Bethlehem Chapel. Hus became the movement's leading representative, and was condemned as a heretic by the Council of Constance and burned at the stake.

The Hussite movement soon became divided between a moderate Prague party, headed from 1429 by Jan Rokycana (c.1390-1471), the priest of the Týn Church on Prague's Old Town Square, and a more radical (and eventually armed) party, the Taborites, based in the new city of Tábor. The Prague party was induced to ally itself with the Catholic Church, and in 1434 their combined forces defeated the Taborite army. Rokycana's election as Archbishop of Prague by a national synod in 1435 was never confirmed by Rome, but by adopting the *Compactata* of 1436 the Council of Basel conceded within Bohemia the chief Hussite demand – communion in both kinds. (This was done against the Pope's wishes, and Pius II cancelled the *Compactata* in 1462.) Henceforward the Bohemian Church (called 'Utraquist' because of its communion in both kinds) enjoyed considerable local self-government under Rokycana. By 1452 the Taborites

---

[1] This account is based chiefly on R. Říčan, *The History of the Bohemian Brethren* (Prague, 1957), Eng. tr. C.D. Crews (Bethlehem, Pennsylvania, 1992) and A. Molnár, 'Die Böhmische Brüderunität. Abriss ihrer Geschichte' in M.P. van Buijtenen, C. Dekker and H. Leeuwenberg (eds), *Unitas Fratrum. Herrnhuter Studien / Moravian Studies* (Utrecht, 1975).

had completely submitted to Rokycana and the Hussite political leader George Poděbrady.

As a church leader Rokycana was moderate and eirenic, but his preaching was characterized by the eschatological urgency of his attacks on what he saw as the moral decline around him. In the 1450s his regular congregation in the Týn Church included a group of young idealists led by his nephew Gregory (d.1474). Inspired by Rokycana's preaching, they sought after the purity and certainty which the established Church he led could not offer, so he sent them to Chelčice to join the radical preacher Peter Chelčický and his followers, the Brethren of Chelčický. Taking his stand on the Bible, Chelčický rejected most of the traditions and practices of the Catholic Church, but he also differed from the Taborites, principally in his rejection of their recourse to armed force. Chelčický advocated social equality, and was critical of secular society, arguing that Christians should neither hold office in it nor be lords.

The Brethren of the Law of Christ

Members of the 'Týn Circle' withdrew from the world to live individually or in small groups in the countryside, first in Bohemia and then in Moravia as well. Gregory, an ascetic with a magnetic personality and gifts of leadership and organization, held them together. In 1458 the main group of these Brethren of the Law of Christ (as they came to be called) settled in Kunvald (Kunwald), near Žamberk (Senftenberg) in north-eastern Bohemia, because they regarded Michael, Žamberk's Utraquist priest, as a 'good priest' to whose care they could confidently entrust themselves. Various other groups in Bohemia and Moravia, including some Waldensians, joined Gregory's movement. The Brethren's simple worship, but still more their private meetings, strict discipline and rejection of oaths, soon provoked opposition and suspicion. George Poděbrady, by now king and seeking to conciliate Rome, inaugurated a period of persecution in the early 1460s. Those imprisoned included, briefly, Michael and Gregory. Some were tortured to force them to recant. The experience of community life far from Prague, and even more the experience of persecution, bound the Brethren together and increased their separation from the rest of the Hussite movement. In 1464 they formulated an Agreement in the Rychnov (Reichenau) Mountains, regulating their common life.

The Synod of Lhotka (1467)

Under Gregory's leadership, the Brethren increasingly rejected the Roman Church and its priesthood. They looked around for another church from whom they could seek ordination of priests, but found none which they regarded as sufficiently pure. They therefore decided to complete their separation from Rome by instituting a new order of priests of their own.[2] To this end, about sixty people gathered in Lhotka in 1467. After electing twenty elders to administer the congregations, they chose nine candidates suitable for ordination to the priesthood and prepared twelve slips of paper, writing the word *'jest'* ('it is he') on three of them. Each candidate was given one slip of paper, drawn as a lot, so allowance was made for the possibility that no priests should be chosen. In fact the three positive lots were drawn. Of the three men thus selected, Matthias of Kunvald was chosen to have 'the first place'. This institution of a separate priesthood at the Synod of Lhotka marked the definitive establishment of the *Unitas Fratrum* (Unity of the Brethren), also known as the Church of the Bohemian Brethren.

For some, including Gregory, election by the congregation and selection by the lot constituted sufficient ordination, but others protested against this view. It was therefore agreed that they should be 'confirmed' in their priesthood by laying on of hands, but then the question arose, by whom this should be done. Some suggested ordination by Michael, who was a priest in Roman orders. The Brethren were agreed that in the New Testament there was no essential difference between episcopate and presbyterate; for them, the difference was one of task, not of order. The fact that Michael was not a bishop was therefore not a concern. Others objected to Michael's Roman orders; the Brethren's ordinations were intended to mark a break from what they saw as the corruption of the Roman Church. These preferred to seek ordination from the Waldensians,

---

[2] This account of the ordinations is based principally on J.T. Müller, *Geschichte der Böhmischen Brüder*, i (Herrnhut, 1922), pp.113-148. For an earlier Anglican examination, see the *Report of the Committee appointed by the Archbishop of Canterbury to consider the Orders of the Unitas Fratrum or Moravians* (Cambridge, [1907]), which made use of Müller's *Das Bischoftum der Brüder-Unität* (Herrnhut, 1889). The most recent account is A. Molnár, 'Bratrsky Synod ve Lhotce u Rychnova', in A. Molnár, R. Říčan and M. Flegl (eds), *Bratrsky Sborník* (Prague, 1967), pp.15-37. I am indebted to the Revd Dr Johann Schneider for translating the most important sections of the latter for me.

as representing a purer stream. The course chosen did justice to both these views. Michael was consecrated bishop by a Waldensian elder (who has not been identified) and in turn consecrated Matthias bishop. Matthias then ordained the other two as priests. Michael then laid down both his Roman and Waldensian orders and was ordained by Matthias. Ecumenical considerations (notably a desire not to offend against Utraquist sensibilities) were a key factor in the decision to obtain 'confirmation' of the new priesthood from a source outside the Unity, but the ordinations were clearly seen as a new start. As a further mark of this, it would appear that the Brethren were then re-baptized by the new priests. For over sixty years, converts to the Unity continued to be re-baptized.

The Waldensians did not possess the 'apostolic succession' as traditionally understood, and in any case, the Brethren rejected this and wanted nothing to do with it. In obtaining ordination from the Waldensian elder they neither intended to acquire the sign of the historic episcopate nor believed that they had done so. However, the method adopted for 'confirming' the ordinations indicates that the Brethren shrank from beginning an entirely new ministry modelled on the primitive Church but with no connection to that of other churches past or present. 'Let no one think', they wrote in 1471, 'that we devised something new at this election and ordination.'[3] They saw the Waldensians as standing in a succession of apostolic teaching and apostolic life in humility, poverty and willingness to suffer, which they believed could be traced from the primitive Church. It was to this stream of apostolicity that they sought to connect themselves by seeking ordination from the Waldensian elder.[4] Although they neither sought nor received the sign of the historic episcopate, they did desire to stand in what might be called an apostolic succession of teaching and life stemming from the primitive Church.

Persecution, Growth and Transition

Separation from the Utraquist Church resulted in some places in the arrest of Brethren and their imprisonment as schismatics and heretics. Some were tortured, some starved to death, one burned. In 1471,

---

[3] *Report of the Committee* (1907), p.23.

[4] Müller, *Geschichte der Böhmischen Brüder,* i, 147.

however, Vladislav Jagielo became king and declared an anmesty. Years of peace and growth followed. Congregations were established, in Moravia as well as in Bohemia, under the protection of favourable noblemen, and in 1480 several hundred Waldensians from Brandenburg migrated to Bohemia and Moravia to form German-speaking congregations of the Unity. By now the Unity had between one and two thousand members. Persecution resumed in Moravia in 1481, however, when King Matthias Corvinus of Hungary, to whom Moravia had been ceded three years earlier, ordered the Brethren there to emigrate. This was the first of many occasions when members of the Unity were forced into exile. Those who left found refuge in Moldavia, but their banishment was soon rescinded and they gradually returned.

Under Chelčický's and Gregory's inspiration, the Brethren rejected city life and many of the trades associated with it. They avoided involvement in public affairs (including office-holding and the exercise of authority), refused oaths and military service, and recommended 'plain dress and frugal food'. However, in the early 1470s a number of theologically educated converts joined Gregory in literary activity, defending and promoting the Unity. This aroused interest among educated people, in the cities and amongst the nobility. Notable converts included a nobleman, Jan Kostka (by 1480), and a group of Prague students, among them Lukás Černy (c.1458-1528), a native of Prague who joined the Unity soon after his graduation in 1481. It was intensive reading of Peter Chelčický that brought Lukás into the Unity, but in the long run the accession of scholars, town-dwellers and nobles was to change the Unity's direction fundamentally, leading it away from many of Chelčický's teachings.

After Gregory died in 1474, Matthias of Kunwald continued to preside over the Unity as its bishop *(Senior)* until his own death in 1500. A council of elders (both priests and laymen), later called the Inner Council (Úzká Rada) to distinguish it from the Synod or wider council, was chosen to advise him. An office of deacon was very quickly established alongside that of priest, and by 1490 there were lay 'helpers' and 'judges'. In 1478 infant baptism was accepted – those baptized within the Unity as infants were received into the congregation by confirmation – but the rebaptism of adult converts persisted until the 1530s. Married men were ordained to the priesthood, but once ordained, priests were not allowed to marry.

From soon after Gregory's death the Brethren's early emphasis on seeking salvation by good works, righteousness and renunciation of the world had begun to be questioned by those who wished to place more emphasis on justification by faith alone. This theological dispute had practical consequences, for if faith were all-important, the early rigour of the Brethren's rejection of city life and secular engagement might be relaxed without harmful spiritual consequences. It was the practical questions that eventually came to a head.[5] Increasingly, town-dwellers and nobles sought reception into the Unity, while the devastating incursions of Matthias Corvinus led members in the countryside to seek refuge in the towns. Brethren came under increasing pressure to fulfil the obligations of membership of the secular community (holding office, taking oaths, etc). A congregation having been formed in Litomysl (Leitomischl), its members felt in 1490 that they should be willing to assume municipal offices. Some felt that by becoming involved in civic life the Brethren could exert a positive influence on it, but the majority of the Inner Council wished to uphold the Unity's original stance. A synod held in 1494 finally decided in favour of secular involvement. Matthias was persuaded to remain in office, but as bishop retained only the power of ordination, actual leadership passing to Procopius Ryšavý (a graduate who had joined the Unity in the early 1470s) as Judge of the Unity and Chairman of the Inner Council. The new Inner Council ruled that Brethren might now live by trades formerly considered questionable (except banking). A declaration signed, among others, by Michael and the three original priests declared that they would no longer be bound by Gregory's and Chelčický's writings. This transition was not achieved painlessly; a minority party seceded, establishing its own priesthood in 1500, and did not die out until the 1540s.

The Era of Lukás of Prague (1494-1528)

From 1494 Lukás Černy came increasingly to dominate the Unity. Significantly, he was the priest of a town congregation, that in Mladá Boleslav (Jungbunzlau), which under his leadership came to be regarded as the Unity's centre. In about one hundred publications he gave the

---

[5] These are discussed in A. Molnár, 'Die Auseinandersetzung zwischen der kleinen und der großen Partei der Alten Brüder-Unität', *Unitas Fratrum*, viii (1980), 49-58.

Unity a new theological basis, which was then embodied in the decisions of synods in the later 1490s. A revised consitution for the *Unitas Fratrum*, agreed in 1499, similarly displayed Lukás' influence. The lay element in the Inner Council and synods decreased, preventing the nobles who were increasingly joining the Unity from exerting excessive influence. Following Matthias's death in 1500, four bishops (*seniors*) were chosen: the two others who were ordained priest in 1467, Lukás, and a fourth. Each was assigned an area to administer (two in Bohemia, two in Moravia), and they took turns to ordain and preside at assemblies. In 1499 the Inner Council and Matthias had given the two priests of 1467 authority to ordain, but this does not seem to have been regarded as amounting to consecration as bishops; nonetheless, following the election of the four new bishops these two consecrated the other two. Liturgies for the ordination of bishops, priests and deacons were approved in 1501. These too may be credited to Lukás, and hymnals published in 1505 and 1519 are also associated with him.

Barely had the Unity been established on its new footing before a fresh wave of persecution broke upon it. In 1503 a royal decree banned the Brethren from holding public meetings and ordered punishment of heretics found in the royal cities. Six Brethren were burned and others imprisoned. In 1508 the so-called Mandate of St James, banning the meetings and publications of heretics, was enacted. The Brethren argued that the law did not apply to them, as they were not heretics, and it was not rigorously enforced, but they were obliged to ensure that public activities were conducted inconspicuously. During this period one layman was burned and one priest was imprisoned and starved (though not to death). After the king's death in 1516 royal power was weakened so much that Lukás urged the congregations to resume public worship, which they did without attracting further persecution.

From 1517 the Lutheran Reformation, and soon that of Zwingli, challenged the Brethren to define their position on the presence of Christ in the Eucharist. Lukás held to the traditional Taborite formula, that Christ was present 'sacredly, spiritually, powerfully and truly', and thus steered a middle course between the positions of Luther and Zwingli. Discussions with Luther were held between 1522 and 1524, and from 1525 Zwinglian influence led to a relatively small separation from the Unity. Lukás rejected alliance with either the Swiss or the German Reformations, and discussions with German-speaking Anabaptist congregations established in Moravia from 1526 came to nothing.

The Era of Jan Augusta (1532-1548)

Lukás of Prague died in 1528. He had served as Judge of the Unity (Chairman of the Inner Council) only since 1518, when the last of the priests ordained in 1467 died, but in fact he had been the chief influence on its development for over thirty years. As had happened with Gregory, however, a synod held in 1531 declared that Lukás' writings were not binding. The following year, a younger generation of leaders was elected onto the Inner Council, including Michael Weisse, a German ex-monk from Breslau, and Jan Augusta (1500-72), who was immediately elected a *senior*. Weisse, who died in 1534, is remembered for his hymns, a number of which are still sung in Germany today. These appeared in the German hymnbook, published in 1531, which he compiled for the Unity's German-speaking congregations, Lanškroun (Landskron) and Fulnek. Weisse inclined towards Zürich, Augusta (like several others in the new leadership) towards Lutheranism.

Augusta was only one of four *seniors* (three in Bohemia and one in Moravia), but he soon emerged as the leading figure. He had a sense of mission to the whole Czech nation, and at first strove for closer relations with the Utraquist Church, which he hoped would be purified by the Brethren's influence. (From 1540, however, relations worsened considerably, and polemic flew in both directions.) By now, participation in civic life, including government and justice, was seen as positively good; oaths were accepted, as was military service to defend the nation against the Turks. The public baptism of twelve or more Bohemian noblemen in Mladá Boleslav in September 1530 was of great significance for the Unity's position in Czech national life.

The Unity now came into closer contact with the German Reformation. From 1530 students were sent to Wittenberg and other German cities. In response to requests from Germany, an account of the Brethren's teachings was published. Doubtless as a result of Lutheran influence, the re-baptism of converts was ended. In 1535 two Brethren (probably Augusta and another) visited Wittenberg for a month, returning with commendations of the Unity's faith and order by Luther and

Melanchthon. Also in 1535, a royal decree banished the Brethren from three royal cities; two lords and a priest were imprisoned. In order to secure their release by demonstrating their orthodoxy, the Brethren drew up a Confession of Faith. This was signed by twelve lords and thirty-three knights and presented to King Ferdinand by two further lords. Two emissaries (again probably Augusta and another) took the document to Wittenberg to show it to Luther. Of the German Reformers, however, the Brethren felt closest to the Strasbourg reformer Martin Bucer, with whom they established contact in 1540 through an emissary, the nineteen year old acolyte Matěj Červenka. In 1540 they published a Czech translation of Bucer's *Von der Wahren Seelsorge*. Červenka also brought the Brethren into contact with Calvin, who was in Strasbourg at the time of his visit.

By the mid-1540s the Unity's early austerity was disappearing. Personal discipline was growing lax, and in 1544 Augusta publicly expelled a lord and his chambermaid for adultery over a long period. In this situation, the Inner Council in 1546 (the year of Luther's death) explicitly turned back to the writings of Lukás of Prague, althouth the Unity's doctrine, as it had developed and been expressed under Luther's influence, was not further altered.

Renewed Persecution and New Leaders (1547-1571)

Two of the *seniors* died in 1547, leaving Augusta as one of only two remaining *seniors*. One of those who died, Jan Roh, had been Judge of the Unity since 1532, and Augusta was naturally elected to succeed him in that position. Augusta's influence over the Unity was thus at its peak, but it was soon to end. Bohemian noblemen had seized the opportunity of the War of Schmalkalden (1546-7) to rise against King Ferdinand, brother of the Habsburg Emperor Charles V. Prominent among the leaders of the uprising were noble members of the Unity, and following the Emperor's victory their estates were confiscated. Blaming the Unity for the actions of some of its most prominent members, Ferdinand renewed the 1508 Mandate of St James, and in January 1548 all public activity by the Unity in Bohemia was rendered impossible by a new royal decree. The decrees were rigorously enforced in the cities and estates which the king had confiscated, and these included Mladá Boleslav and a number of the Unity's other main centres. In April Augusta himself was arrested and taken to Prague. After interrogation under torture he was incarcerated. In May 1548 a further decree ordered that those who continued to resist should renounce their heresy or emigrate within six weeks. Many fled – eight hundred members of the Unity went to Prussia, and a number of the sixty Bohemian congregations ceased to exist. Persecution reinforced the tendency to return to the earlier austerity of Lukás of Prague. During a brief respite, public worship resumed in Mladá Boleslav in 1553, and in the following year 'the great *shor*', an imposing new meeting house in classical style (still standing today) was erected there; it was soon forced to close, however.

Since the uprising had occurred only in Bohemia, the royal decrees applied only to that territory. Moravia, where there were eighty or ninety congregations, was unaffected and became the Unity's new centre of gravity, where the Inner Council now met. Augusta's only fellow-*senior*, Mach Sionský, led the exiles in Prussia. He died there in 1551, leaving Augusta, still in prison, as the sole bishop. Before leaving, Sionský had commissioned two brethren by the laying on of hands, giving them power to consecrate a successor in the event of his death, and had given two others the jurisdictional powers of a bishop. The Inner Council now sought Augusta's consent to the election of new *seniors*, but he refused. In February 1553, however, Augusta's communications with the Inner Council were discovered and stopped; the story soon circulated that he had been executed. Meanwhile, the two men given power to consecrate *seniors* had also died. A synod of priests and more experienced deacons was therefore called, and Jan Černý (c.1508-1565) and Matěj Červenka (1521-1569) were elected *seniors* (bishops). They were consecrated by members of the Inner Council, all priests. Augusta was, in fact still alive, but after his release from prison he was not asked to perform any supplementary ordination on those consecrated in the meantime – in the eyes of the Unity, the consecration by priests was sufficient. It is from the 1553 ordinations that the episcopal succession of the *Unitas Fratrum* stems. Černý was elected Judge of the Unity, but (probably in reaction to the dominance of Augusta) it was stressed that the leadership should be collective. Two further seniors, Jan Blahoslav (1523-1571) and Jiří Izrael (1510-1588), were elected and consecrated in 1557. Only in 1559 did Augusta learn of the consecrations. He repudiated them, and relationships with the new Inner Council were strained to breaking point, but after his eventual release from prison in 1564 a reconciliation was effected. Augusta was recognized as joint Judge with Černý, but he was no longer influential. During the sixteen years of his imprisonment, the Unity had moved on.

Of the *seniors*, Černý earned a place in the Unity's history as the founder of its archives, which he gathered and brought into order in Mladá Boleslav, while Červenka published a Czech translation of the psalter. More prominent, however, was Jan Blahoslav, an educated intellectual of Christian humanist disposition who (unlike Lukás and Augusta) had been was brought up in the Unity. Like Červenka, he inclined towards Calvinism. He was responsible for a string of treatises written to explain the Unity's position to other churches and to its own members, for the 1561 hymnbook and for a Czech translation of the New Testament (1564) which remains influential today. He continued Černý's work on the archives, and in his spare time worked on a Czech grammar. As a result of Blahoslav's literary activities, the Unity became a leading component in the cultural life of the Czech nation.

The Polish Branch of the Unity

When the exiles fled from Bohemia to Prussia in 1548, they passed through Poland, where the Reformation was still in its infancy, stopping for a while in Posen (Poznan) and Thorn (Torun). Small congregations gathered around them, to which Brethren travelling between Moravia and Prussia continued to preach. In 1551, at the request of the Posen group, Mach Sionský commissioned Jiří Izrael to visit them regularly, and in 1553 Izrael settled in Posen permanently. Early members in Posen included the mayor of Posen and the lord of nearby Ostroróg. Soon the Unity had fifteen congregations in Poland, mostly in rural towns and villages on the estates of favourable noblemen, and a German congregation, with a school, was established in Lissa (Leszno) around 1558. With Izrael's consecration as a *senior* in 1557, the Unity's presence in Poland was recognized as a permanent one. The Unity now effectively had three branches – Bohemia (with its centre in Mladá Boleslav), Moravia (centred on Ivančice) and Poland (Ostroróg). The convening of a synod of the Polish Brethren in 1560 indicated a certain independent identity for the Unity's Polish branch vis à vis the Unity in Bohemia and Moravia. Its character was also rather different. In many cases, it inherited the parish church, and the priests benefitted from glebe and tithes. Nine nobles were elected as *seniores politici* to look after the Unity's temporal interests in Poland. Also, the marriage of priests (originally forbidden) became commoner in Poland sooner than it did in Bohemia and Moravia. Nonetheless, the Unity remained a single entity, governed by the Inner Council.

Plans for a union with the other nascent Protestant groups in Poland (chiefly the Reformed) were explored from 1555, but came to nothing. The Polish branch of the Unity continued to enjoy generally good relations with the Reformed, and from 1562 onwards it always sent its students to Heidelberg or Switzerland; relations with the Lutherans, by contrast, were often strained. In 1570, however, the Reformed and Lutheran churches and the Unity agreed the Consensus of Sandomir (Sandomierz), which established intercommunion between them. This was supplemented by agreements made in Posen between the Unity and the Lutherans, establishing an interchangeability of ministries: the churches remained separate, but agreed not to entice away each other's ministers or congregations; anyone excluded from membership of one church would not be received into the other. The fact that the Unity was established in Poland before the Lutheran and Reformed churches were organized there, and already had a developed church order, gave it a prominence in Poland which it lacked in Bohemia and Moravia.

Calvinism, the Bohemian Confession and the Kralitz Bible

The Unity's closeness to the Reformed in Poland foreshadowed its overall development in a Calvinist direction. In 1574 those of its adherents who were still in Prussia were ordered by the authorities to conform completely to Lutheranism. Most chose instead to return to their homelands or migrate to Poland. From that year, Wittenberg and other Lutheran universities were closed to the Unity's students, so from then on all its students who went abroad studied in the Reformed universities of Western Germany and Switzerland. Many features of Calvinism were congenial to the Brethren. Both traditions had a strong sense of the dominance of God's will and saw the Church as the society of the elect; both emphasized order and discipline in the congregation and gave offices in it to laypeople; both had deliberately broken with catholic liturgical tradition (though in the time of Lukás of Prague, the Unity's worship had become less austere). Although the Brethren remained unwilling to define the nature of Christ's presence in the Eucharist, they felt closest to Calvin's understanding, and the Calvinist churches' greater independence from secular authority again made the Brethren feel closer to them than to the Lutheran churches. These affinities meant that by 1580 Calvinism was the predominant theological tendency in the Unity.

In Bohemia, however, there was also a greater closeness to the Utraquists and the increasingly Lutheran 'neo-Utraquists'. In 1575 the Bohemian Parliament, which included lords and knights who were Brethren, drew up and presented to the Emperor a Bohemian Confession, in whose preparation the Unity shared. The Brethren adhered to it, but it was agreed that they would nonetheless retain their own church order and confession. This alliance brought protection from other nobles, which enabled them to open a series of *sbors* in places where this had not been possible for almost thirty years. It was partly in order to avoid jeopardizing these closer relationships within Bohemia that, despite its increasing Calvinism, the Unity did not allow itself to become identified as belonging to the Reformed family. To do so would also have been dangerous, since the Reformed confession had no legal status within the Empire. Calvinism continued to gain ground in the Unity, however. The chief opposition to this tendency came from Simeon Theofil Turnovský (1544-1608), *Senior* and Judge of the Polish congregations from 1587. Although the Polish Unity enjoyed a close relationship with the Reformed churches there for which there was no parallel in Bohemia and Moravia, Turnovský was also determined to maintain the three-cornered unity of the Consensus of Sandomir, and if the Unity adhered to Calvinism that would imperil relations with the Polish Lutherans.

It was in the last quarter of the sixteenth century that the Brethren's greatest legacy to the Czech people was created. Between 1579 and 1594 the Unity published a six-volume revised edition of the Czech Bible in Kralice (Kralitz). For generations the language of this Kralitz Bible was to be regarded as the standard of pure Czech.

Resurgent Roman Catholicism

Meanwhile, the Counter-Reformation was underway in Bohemia and Moravia. Jesuits had been active there since 1556, and in 1561 the archiepiscopal see of Prague had been restored. Roman Catholic publications attacked the Brethren, and one of the grounds of attack was that they did not have the apostolic succession. In response, the Unity's apologists claimed that in 1467 its first priests had received orders derived from a Roman bishop, and that there had subsequently been an unbroken succession of episcopal consecrations. As has been shown, these claims did not match the historical facts.

In 1584 the Mandate of St James was renewed. Jesuits were brought in by some lords to re-catholicize their estates. Some of the Unity's noble members converted to Roman Catholicism, and several congregations lost the noble protection on which they had depended for survival. Most seriously, Mladá Boleslav, the Unity's Bohemian centre, fell under Roman Catholic rule in 1588. In 1595 it became a royal city, but this was to have fateful consequences when the Mandate was again renewed in 1602. The *shor* was closed and all of the Unity's buildings in Mladá Boleslav were confiscated.

In Poland, too, renewed Roman Catholic confidence resulted in an exodus of noblemen from the Unity. Roman Catholic priests replaced those of the Brethren as parish priests on these estates, and the allegiance of the peasants was lost to the Unity with that of their lords. Protestantism in general was already in retreat when acts of violence against Protestants began. In 1605 both of the Brethren's churches in Posen were burned, and when these churches, together with the Lutheran church, were destroyed in 1616, the Brethren fled. About a year earlier, the Reformed in the Kujav area had lost their central church and seminary in Radziejów. Reduced to just seven congregations, they made overtures to the Unity. It, too, was much weakened, and agreed to a union, which was completed at a synod in Ostroróg in 1627. The Reformed *Senior* became an additional *senior* of the Unity, and in time became its leader in Poland. (The separate and larger Reformed churches in Lesser Poland and Lithuania were unaffected by this union in Greater Poland.) These developments, together with the adherence to the Unity of a large number of Scottish merchants and their families, who had settled in Polish cities, inevitably increased its Calvinist leanings.

Last Flowering in Bohemia (1609-1620)

In 1609 the Emperor Rudolf II was forced to sign the Letter of Majesty, granting toleration to the Bohemian Protestants on the basis of the Bohemian Confession. The Brethren insisted on retaining their own priesthood, liturgy, church order and discipline, but a single twelve-member consistory was to be established for the Utraquists, the Lutherans and the Unity, making an eventual union likely. The Unity was at last allowed to hold public worship in Prague, and was given use of the Bethlehem Chapel, Hus's preaching place, as a gesture of goodwill. In response, the Brethren's priests began to wear albs when conducting services. Public worship was resumed in Mladá Boleslav and elsewhere. During this period the Unity produced a wealth of publications – the complete Kralitz Bible (1613), the liturgy, the catechism, hymnbooks, prayer books and works of theology. The Unity's most promising young scholar was Jan Amos Komenský (Comenius) (1592-1670), who was ordained in 1618 and became priest of the Fulnek congregation in Moravia. Comenius was to become the Unity's most famous bishop, an educationalist and thinker of international importance.

Especially in Moravia, however, the Unity was in numerical decline. Union with the other Protestant churches meant that it was distinguished only by its church order and stricter discipline. This led at first to an exodus of members and fewer conversions, and in time to a relaxation of the Unity's moral demands.

The End of the Unity in Bohemia and Moravia (1620-1628)

Continued Roman Catholic aggression led eventually to the choice of Frederick V, the Elector Palatine of the Rhine, as King of Bohemia in place of the Emperor Ferdinand II. Frederick was crowned on 31 October 1619 by the Utraquist Administrator and the Brethren's *Senior*. The 'Winter King' reigned only for one year, however, and his defeat by Ferdinand at the Battle of the White Mountain on 8 November 1620 signalled the end of the Unity in Bohemia and Moravia, and indeed of Czech Protestantism altogether. Among the twenty-seven Czech lords, knights and burghers who were executed on Prague's Old Town Square on

21 June 1621 were seven Brethren. The suppression of Protestantism began immediately, and in 1624 all Protestant clergy (including those of the Unity, who numbered around two hundred) were banished from Bohemia and Moravia. Nobles and burghers were forced to choose between exile and conversion to Roman Catholicism, but for the rest of the population there was no choice at all; they were forcibly converted.

By 1628 between five and six thousand Brethren had gone into exile. One of the last to do so was Comenius, who left for Poland in February 1628 with around one thousand refugees. Most of the Bohemians took refuge in Poland, while the majority from Moravia went to Slovakia. An exile congregation was also founded in Brieg (Brzeg) in Silesia. Many Bohemians settled across the border in Saxony, and educated Brethren were scattered throughout Germany and Holland, wherever they could find employment.

The Unity in Poland

In Poland, the Czech Brethren remained organizationally distinct from the Polish Unity, hoping to be able to return home in due course. Their centre was Lissa (Lezno), to whose original German congregation a small Polish congregation had been attached. Here Comenius settled, and here the Unity's printing press, brought from Kralitz, was set up. In October 1632 the Czech branch of the Unity held a synod in Lissa, and elected two *seniors* for Bohemia and two for Moravia. One of the latter was Comenius.

Increasing Roman Catholic pressure on the Reformed in Lesser Poland and Lithuania led them too to seek union with the Polish Unity in Greater Poland. This was achieved in 1634, on the basis of the Unity's church order. The churches effectively formed a federation, with a separate administration in each of the three territories. This development naturally gave further impetus to the Unity's development in a Reformed direction. In 1637 the Polish Unity lost Ostroróg, and its seminary and *Senior* moved to Lissa.

The Czech Brethren's hopes of returning to Bohemia and Moravia were dashed by the Peace of Westphalia in 1648, which left the Czech lands completely under Habsburg control. Comenius had been absent in

England (1641-2) and in Elbing, on the Baltic coast (1642-8), but being now the only surviving *senior* of the Bohemian and Moravian branch of the Unity, he returned to Lissa. In 1650 he visited the Moravian exiles in Slovakia, who had similarly attached themselves to the Reformed Church in 1644/7.

Further disaster struck Lissa in 1656, when it was burned by the Swedes. Comenius lost all his possessions, including his library and manuscripts representing forty years' work. He and other Brethren found refuge in Silesia. By now 64, he moved to safety in Amsterdam. Lissa was rebuilt in 1658, but only a part of the Czech exiles returned. In 1662 a synod was held, at which, with Comenius' written consent, the one surviving Polish *senior* consecrated Comenius's son-in-law Peter Jablonsky Figulus (1619-70) as *Senior* of the Czech branch of the Unity. In 1666 Figulus became the Reformed court preacher in Memel (Klaipeda), where he died in 1670. Comenius, who died on 15 November that year, was thus after all the last bishop of the Czech branch of the Unity. In 1700 a sermon in Czech was preached in Lissa for the last time. Not long after Comenius's death, the Counter-Reformation in Hungary led to the seizure of the Brethren's churches in Slovakia; their congregations were dispersed.

Thus the Polish Unity alone remained, with fifteen congregations centred on Lissa (where the main congregation was German, with a weaker Polish congregation attached). Nicholas Gertich, pastor of the congregation in Brieg, had been consecrated *Senior* of the Polish Unity in 1662, and the succession was maintained. In 1699 Figulus's son (and Comenius's grandson) Daniel Ernst Jablonski (1660-1741), the Reformed court chaplain in Berlin, was consecrated *Senior* of the Polish Unity. It was he who in 1735 and 1737, with the written consent of his fellow-*senior* Christian Sitkovius, consecrated the first bishops of the Moravian Church, sealing its inheritance of the identity and traditions of the *Unitas Fratrum*.

In 1768, when only ten (German and Polish) congregations remained, the Polish Unity finally achieved religious freedom and security. It had long gone over to the Reformed confession, retaining little more than the name of the Unity and ordination by *seniors* in the succession which had been maintained unbroken since the mid-sixteenth century. In 1841, when there were just five congregations left, the *Senior* died without consecrating a successor. Bishops of the Moravian Church stepped in and consecrated a bishop for the Polish Unity in 1844 (and again in 1868). The Polish Unity survived in small numbers, enjoying good relations with the renewed Unity in Herrnhut, until World War II finally extinguished it.

THE MORAVIAN CHURCH

Although the *Unitas Fratrum* was suppressed in Bohemia and Moravia in the 1620s, it was not extinguished. Deprived of clergy and of aristocratic leaders, laypeople nonetheless continued to meet in secret to read the Bible and other books and to sing and pray together.[1] In 1661 Comenius published a German hymnbook and catechism for the remnants of his old congregaion in Fulneck and the surrounding villages in the Kuhländel, a German-speaking area of northern Moravia close to the Silesian border. One hundred years later, this 'hidden seed' came to life as a result of an evangelical revival centred on the Lutheran Jesus Church in Teschen (Cieszyn), Silesia. The Roman Catholic authorities responded with renewed and severe persecution, and in 1722 this impelled three young men from Sehlen (Zilina) and their families to leave Moravia with Christian David (1692-1751), the revivalist preacher who had awakened them, seeking a place where they could practise their religion more freely. They were permitted to settle on the estate of Count Nikolaus Ludwig von Zinzendorf (1700-1760) in Upper Lusatia, Saxony, and on 17 June 1722 Christian David felled the first tree for their settlement, which they named Herrnhut. These first Moravian exiles were soon joined by others, including in 1724 five men from Zauchtenthal (Suchdol nad Odrou), one of the villages near Fulnek, who were conscious of their identity as heirs of the *Unitas Fratrum*, whose traditions had been handed down in their families.

By April 1727 the population of Herrnhut had reached 220, and was still growing. Divisions amongst the Moravian exiles – and disputes between those who tended to Calvinism and the strongly Lutheran pastor of Berthelsdorf, the parish in which Herrnhut was situated – were exacerbated by the fact that one third of Herrnhut's adult population had come from various other parts of Germany.[2] Zinzendorf therefore took up residence

---

[1] See A. Vacovsky, 'History of the Hidden Seed (1620-1722)' in M.P. van Buijtenen, C. Dekker and H. Leeuwenberg (eds), *Unitas Fratrum. Herrnhuter Studien / Moravian Studies* (Utrecht, 1975).

[2] For sources and further information on the period to 1760, see C.J. Podmore, 'The Role of the Moravian Church in England: 1728-1760' (D.Phil., Oxford, 1994). The most recent history of the Moravian Church internationally is J.T. and K.G. Hamilton, *History of the Moravian Church. The Renewed Unitas Fratrum 1722-1957* (Bethlehem, Pa., 1967). Although in need of correction at some points in the light of more recent work, A.J. Lewis, *Zinzendorf the Ecumenical Pioneer* (London, 1962) remains the best study of Zinzendorf in English.

in Herrnhut in order to try to bring order to the developing Christian community, for which he issued secular and spiritual statutes and instituted 'bands' (fellowship groups). He then studied Comenius' accounts of the discipline and practices of the *Unitas Fratrum*, discovering striking similarities with the system he had established for Herrnhut. All of these factors contributed to renewal and spiritual growth, which culminated on 13 August 1727, when the congregation gathered for Holy Communion in the parish church in Berthelsdorf and experienced a new unity in the Spirit. This experience completed and sealed the inauguration of the new community of Herrnhut.

Beginning in 1727, the Herrnhut community soon sought to establish bonds of fellowship with Christians in other cities, lands and churches and sent messengers to tell them of the founding of Herrnhut and the events there, in which they believed God had acted. Thus ecumenical fellowship was a priority from the outset. In 1728 the custom of identifying a scriptural *Losung* ('watchword' or daily text) for each day began. Since 1731 these have been published for each year in advance, and they now appear in over forty languages. The *Losungen* are used very widely by German Protestants, and the German language edition alone amounts to over 1,200,000 copies each year. This gives the Moravian Church an influence in German church life out of all proportion to its numbers.

As early as 1732, the first missionaries were sent out from Herrnhut to the West Indies, and missions to Greenland (1733), Surinam (1733), South Africa (1737) and Ceylon (1739) followed. The Moravians were therefore among the pioneers of Protestant missions. Pressure on Saxony from the Habsburg authorities, angered at the exodus of population from Bohemia and Moravia, combined with increasing unease on the part of the Saxon government at the development in Herrnhut, made the position of the Bohemian and Moravian refugees there uncertain. Settlements were therefore established in North America – first in Georgia (1735-1740), and subsequently in Pennsylvania (1741). It was in the hope that the orders of missionaries ordained by a bishop of the *Unitas Fratrum* would be recognized in the British colonies that Jablonski was asked to consecrate a bishop for the Herrnhut community. His consecration in 1735 of the carpenter David Nitschmann, one of the 1724 Moravian exiles, as a bishop of the *Unitas Fratrum* set the seal on the Herrnhut community's inheritance of its identity and traditions. Zinzendorf himself was consecrated a bishop in 1737. A further step in the appropriation of the traditions of the *Unitas Fratrum* was taken in July 1745, when a General Synod decided to revive the lay office of acolyte and the distinction between the orders of deacon and presbyter.

Zinzendorf's banishment from Saxony in 1736 led to the establishment of communities in Wetteravia (north-east of Frankfurt am Main), notably Herrnhaag (1738-1750). Moravians[3] travelled to the Caribbean and North America through the Netherlands and England, and in both countries people were attracted to them. This resulted in the establishment in the Netherlands of first a community (1736) and then a fully-fledged settlement, Zeist (1746). In 1738 Peter Böhler (1712-1775) founded a Herrnhut-style band in London. This grew into the Fetter Lane Society, which in 1739 and 1740 was to be the hub of the Evangelical Revival in England. In 1741 a group of Moravians was sent to London at the Society's request to take over its leadership. In 1742 the first English Moravian congregation was established to take charge of societies established by the Yorkshire evangelist Benjamin Ingham, and a second congregation was formed out of the Fetter Lane Society.[4] Other notable English evangelists – Jacob Rogers, David Taylor and John Cennick – also gave their societies (in Bedfordshire, Cheshire and Wiltshire respectively) into the Moravians' care. As a Moravian, John Cennick was to lay the foundations for the Moravian Church's significant presence in Ireland. All the Moravian congregations worldwide remained part of the single Moravian Church, which can therefore be said to have been the first international protestant church.

Zinzendorf envisaged the body which had thus grown out of the Herrnhut community as an interdenominational fellowship of Christians, most of whom would continue as members of their own churches. He was opposed to proselytism in Christian countries, while deeply committed to

---

[3] The church into which the Herrnhut community grew came to be known in English as 'the Moravian Church', because the exiles who founded Herrnhut came from Moravia. By 1756 (when the vast majority of members were not of Czech descent), there were still 1,014 living members of Moravian stock as against 629 of Bohemian descent. Except where the context indicates otherwise, the term 'Moravian' is used hereinafter to denote members of the Moravian Church, regardless of their origins or descent.

[4] For the London Congregation, see C.J. Podmore (ed.), *The Fetter Lane Moravian Congregation,* London, 1742-1992 (London, 1992).

mission amongst the heathen. The dominance of these ecumenical and missionary concerns explains both the very small size of the Moravian Church in Europe and its relative numerical strength outside Europe. In 1744 Zinzendorf developed his *Tropenidee* (*Tropus* concept), whereby only ministers and full-time church workers, congregations in the mission field and actual Czech exiles and their descendants would be reckoned as belonging to the Moravian Church proper. This would be one of the 'tropes' or branches of a *Brüdergemeine* (Unity or Congregation of the Brethren), which would also comprise Lutheran and Reformed tropes under the oversight of clergy of the respective confessions. It proved impossible to maintain this distinction, and in most countries the Moravian Church became a separate church alongside the existing denominations. In German Zinzendorf's preferred name, *die Brüdergemeine*, was retained, but in English the name 'Moravian Church' eventually won through.

In Switzerland, however, where Moravian work dates from 1738, the members of Moravian societies remain members of the cantonal Reformed churches and have always understood their role as that of a community serving the cantonal church ('als Dienstgemeinschaft der Landeskirche verpflichtet'). In the Baltic territories (modern Estonia and Latvia), where Moravian work commenced in 1737, the members of Moravian societies similarly remained within the Lutheran churches. With a membership of 83,000 by 1857, the Moravian societies there exerted very significant influence on the development of the Estonian and Latvian churches during the eighteenth and nineteenth centuries.

Zinzendorf has been described as the greatest German theologian between Luther and Schleiermacher, but commentators disagree about the interpretation of his stance, variously representing him as standing within the Pietist, Lutheran, Mystic and Enlightenment traditions. He grew up in Pietist circles within the Lutheran Church of Saxony, and was educated under August Hermann Francke at Halle, but from 1733 the Hallensian Pietists opposed the Moravians. Zinzendorf was, of course, a member of the Lutheran Church of Saxony, and always regarded himself as a Lutheran. From 1734 he turned to Luther as his chief inspiration, but his thought bore the clear impression of mystic and enlightenment influences.

In 1741 Leonhard Dober resigned as Chief Elder (*Generalälteste*) of the Moravian Church, an office which he had held since 1733. The fact that his decision came shortly before Zinzendorf's departure on an extended visit to America made the question of a successor all the more difficult. A synodical conference held in Red Lion Square, London, on 16 September was unable to identify a successor and instead decided that the Saviour himself should henceforth be the Chief Elder. This decision was proclaimed to all the congregations on 13 November, and that day is still kept as the Memorial Day of the Realization of the Headship of Christ. The belief in Christ's headship of the Church gave the Moravians a strong awareness of His presence among them; indeed for some years after Zinzendorf's return in 1743 one chair was left empty at conferences as a reminder of His presence. Moravian theology and piety remains strongly christocentric, and the characteristic Moravian emphasis on collegiality in church government can also be traced to the 1741 decision.

From Zinzendorf's return from America in 1743 until about 1750 Moravian spirituality reached a peak retrospectively referred to as 'the Sifting Time'. It was christocentric, focusing on Christ's blood and wounds and on Christ as the husband of Christians, and towards the end of the decade became increasingly centred on the Eucharist. Moravians aimed at becoming ever more childlike and simple, playing games and developing a language laced with diminutive terms of endearment. It was in the Moravian hymns of these years that this spirituality found its most controversial expression. These developments provoked growing public criticism and ridicule, which left the Moravians chastened and repentant. The nineteenth century saw this as a time of 'pathological deformation' in Zinzendorf's teaching, but despite its undoubted excesses, it is now recognized as not an aberration, but Zinzendorf's most creative period, continuous with his previous development and in its essentials not rejected in the settled maturity of his last decade. It is no co-incidence that for the Moravian Church the 1740s was a period of unparalleled growth and vigour.

Zinzendorf was also original and creative in the area of liturgy, giving the Moravian Church a strong but distinctive tradition of worship which was neither derived from the Western Catholic tradition nor marked by an absence of liturgical form. Moravian worship remains distinctive, although it has been influenced to varying degrees in each province by the worship of the larger churches in the countries concerned.[5]

After Zinzendorf's death in 1760, his colleague August Gottlieb Spangenberg (1704-1792) came to dominate the Moravian Church. A General Synod held in 1764 gave the Moravian Church a constitution. It was to remain a single unit, governed by a General Synod and, between synods, by a *Directorium* elected by the Synod and accountable to it, with separate boards responsible for civil and financial affairs. The next General Synod, meeting in 1769, substituted for the three central boards a Unity Elders' Conference (UEC) composed of three departments. The provincial boards in Britain and America became 'helpers' or agents of the UEC, appointed by and responsible to the UEC rather than the congregations they supervised. All Moravian missions were supervised by a committee of three brethren in Herrnhut, and the schools by six trustees. The 1775 General Synod intensified this centralization by making the minister the agent and representative of the UEC and increasing the UEC's financial control over the congregations.

In his *Life of Zinzendorf* (1772-5) and his *Idea Fidei Fratrum* (1779), Spangenberg effectively redefined the Moravian Church's doctrinal position, presenting Zinzendorf and the Moravian Church as representatives of protestant orthodoxy. Christian Gregor's 1778 hymnbook re-wrote Moravian hymnody on the same lines. During the period from 1760 to 1900, the predominant spirit in the Moravian Church was one of cautious conservatism. In 1900 its membership on the European Continent stood at 7,781, compared with 7,860 in 1800. Its life was concentrated in settlement congregations villages in which, at least in the earlier part of the period, only members of the church were permitted to reside permanently or own property, and which therefore inevitably developed a certain inward-looking quality. Moravians during this 'period of the settlement congregation', have been characterized as 'the quiet in the land'.

This description needs qualification, however. The Moravian Church exerted influence beyond its confines through three 'works': mission, education and the 'diaspora'. The scale of its overseas missions, with

---

[5] For Moravian worship in England, see F. Linyard and P. Tovey, *Moravian Worship* (Grove Worship Series, 129, 1994).

95,424 members in 1900, was very great indeed in comparison with the numerical strength of the 'home' church, and the Moravian Church continues to play a significant role in consortia of mission agencies. The overseas missionary enterprise of the Moravian Church, unlike that of other churches, has never been directed through a missionary society. It has always been regarded as the responsibility of the whole Moravian Church. In the British Province, the Provincial Board is also the Mission Board. On the European Continent the Moravian Church maintained about thirty boarding schools in the nineteenth century, so that many from outside the church came to experience the life of its settlement congregations through their own education in them or that of their children. In England and Ireland there were no fewer than ten girls' and five boys' schools, of which schools in Fulneck (Yorkshire) and Ockbrook (Derbyshire) survive. Finally, the Moravian Church on the European Continent carried out a substantial 'diaspora' work in twenty districts, visiting individuals and groups who were not members of the Moravian Church. All three 'works' brought new people into membership of the Moravian Church, but this was not their purpose; they were conceived as a service to others. A further means of influence, the 'watchwords', was mentioned above. The revival which began in the Niesky *Pädagogium,* the Unity's elite school, in 1841 also served to redress any lack of vitality.

In Britain and Ireland the picture differed from that on the Continent in several respects. Of the congregations, only Fulneck (Yorkshire), Ockbrook (Derbyshire), Fairfield (Manchester) and Gracehill (Ulster) could be described as settlements, although in London and Bedford the Moravians had complexes of adjacent buildings. Furthermore, these settlements were generally on a somewhat smaller scale and less isolated than those on the Continent. Between 1822 and 1900 a modest rise in membership, from 4,867 to 6,095, was recorded.

During the first half of the nineteenth century resistance grew in America and Britain to the Unity's centralized form of government. The 1848 General Synod delegated full legislative power in purely provincial matters to provincial synods – one for Germany (and neighbouring countries), one for Britain (and Ireland) and two for America (north and south). In 1857 each was allowed to elect its own Provincial Elders' Conference (PEC), although until 1869 the UEC appointed the President of the British PEC and one member of the America (South) PEC. The

General Synod remained the Unity's highest legislative body, with final authority, especially in matters of faith and order, worship and missions, and the UEC remained responsible for matters affecting the Unity as a whole, as well as retaining direct responsibility for the German Province. The Synod further agreed to commence evangelistic work in Bohemia and Moravia with a view to establishing congregations (not just diaspora societies) there. Further constitutional changes were made by the 1899 General Synod. The UEC was replaced by a Unity Directory consisting of the boards of each of the four provinces, together with the mission board. The Directory worked through an executive committee of three and periodic Unity Conferences consisting of one member from each of the provincial boards and two from the mission board. Thus, all of the central structures were now federal in nature, but the Moravian Church remained a single church with a single Unity church order and general synod.

World War I had the effect of increasing the division between the British Province and the Moravian Church on the Continent. In the face of the strong anti-German feeling in Britain, the British Moravians, with their foreign-sounding name, felt obliged to distance themselves from their German roots, and the war broke many ties (for example the practice of sending British children to Moravian schools in Germany) which were not fully restored during the brief and difficult interwar period. Since 1900 the small German Moravian community has produced a considerable number of scholars whose historical and theological work is as remarkable for its quality as for its quantity. Nazi rule and the ensuing World War II in turn left a deep mark on the German (Continental) Province, which lost its six Silesian congregations and now has no residential seminary and just two boarding schools. Despite this, its intellectual vitality has continued. The province was able to retain its unity while Germany was divided, with two boards and two synods functioning under a single provincial church order, and the Herrnhut (Eastern) District played a disproportionately large part in church life in the German Democratic Republic. (The division of the Continental Province into two districts was ended in 1992, following the unification of Germany.)

In 1957 a General Synod met for the first time since 1931. The Unity Church Order was thoroughly revised, and three classes of province were identified: self-governing Unity provinces, synodal provinces with limited self-rule, and associate provinces. The Moravian Church in

Czechoslovakia was recognized as the fifth Unity province, and provision was made for this status to be granted later to further provinces which already had their own synods, and for further provinces to become synodal provinces. Thus began a process whereby all of the mission areas eventually became self-governing. The next General Synod, held in 1967, altered its name to 'Unity Synod' and resolved that in future meetings should be held at seven-yearly intervals. Between meetings of the Unity Synod the Unity Board, which consists of one member of the Provincial Board of each province governed by its own synod, acts as an executive. Today, the Moravian Church consists of nineteen provinces and two Unity undertakings (congregations and refugee work in North India and a home for handicapped Arab children in Palestine).

THE *UNITAS FRATRUM* AND THE CHURCH OF ENGLAND

The Church of the Bohemian Brethren

Fellowship between the Church of England and the *Unitas Fratrum* dates at least from 1641-2, when Jan Amos Comenius (1592-1670), the bishop-in-exile of Czech branch of the Unity, spent nine months in England. Among his English patrons and supporters were several Anglican bishops and clergy, headed by Archbishop Williams of York.[1] Retaining an interest in English ecclesiastical affairs, in 1648 Comenius wrote *Independentia, Aeternarum Confusionum Origo*, a treatise intended to mediate in the controversy raging at that time, in which he admonished all three parties – Episcopalians, Presbyterians and Independents – to moderation and mutual forbearance.[2]

The burning of the Brethren's Polish centre Lissa in 1656 led to the first of a series of appeals for help addressed to the Church in England. Adam Samuel Hartmann (1627-91), pastor of the congregation in Lissa and rector of its grammar school, visited England with Comenius' brother-in-law Paul Cyrill in 1657-8 to raise money for rebuilding of the church, hall and school. They were accompanied by Hartmann's brother Paul, one of Comenius' pupils and a deacon of the *Unitas Fratrum*. He stayed behind, taking his M.A. at Oxford in July 1658. Following the Restoration, Paul Hartmann was ordained priest by Bishop Skinner of Oxford on 16 December 1660.[3] As he was not first ordained deacon (unlike all but three of those ordained priest that day), it would seem that Bishop Skinner recognized his orders. Hartmann was appointed chaplain of Christ Church in 1671 and was rector of Shellingford in Berkshire from 1675 until his death in 1694.

---

[1] For the period 1641-1735, see C.J. Podmore, 'The Role of the Moravian Church in England: 1728-1760' (D.Phil., Oxford, 1994), ch. VII.

[2] M. Spinka, *John Amos Comenius. That Incomparable Moravian* (Chicago, 1943), p.119.

[3] Oxford County Record Office, MS Oxford diocesan papers d.106: Institutions and Ordinations 1660-1702.

The Restoration also prompted Comenius to republish his description of the *Unitas Fratrum's* church order. This won the admiration of significant English churchmen, including Herbert Thorndike (1592-1672) and John Durel (1625-83). In a dedication, Comenius bequeathed to the Church of England the care of his dying church, with these moving and prophetic words:

> To whom shall I leave our possessions? And have we any possessions, when all has been lost? Yes, by God's gift we still own some things which may be willed to others; nor are friends and enemies wanting to whom such things may be left. To our enemies we leave what they have taken from us, or may yet take: our earthly goods – churches, land, schools and the like, and finally, if God, the ruler of all things, should see fit, the lives of those of us who are left; even as it pleased Christ, hanging on the cross, to allow His garments to be divided between the soldiers and Himself to be robbed of his earthly life.
>
> But to you, our friends [the Church of England], we commit, according to the example of the same Divine Master, that which is far better, our dear mother, our Church herself. Take up the care of her now in our stead, whether God will deem her worthy to be revived in her native land, or let her die there and bring her to life again elsewhere. Even in her death, which now seems to be approaching, you ought to love her, because in her life she has gone before you, for over two centuries, with examples of faith and patience.[4]

After a second visit in 1668 in search of donations, Adam Samuel Hartmann visited Oxford again in 1680. By now *Senior* (bishop) of the *Unitas Fratrum* in Poland, he was made an Oxford D.D. and through Archbishop Sancroft and Bishop Compton of London obtained the creation of scholarships at Oxford. The first three scholars included Comenius' grandson Daniel Ernst Jablonski, who studied for three years at Christ Church, becoming closely acquainted with the future Archbishop Wake, then a student of Christ Church. While in England, Jablonski also met Bishops Compton of London and Fell of Oxford. As

---

[4] J.A. Comenius, *De Bono Unitatis et Ordinis, Disciplinaeque ac Obedientiae in Ecclesia recte constituta vel constituenda Ecclesiae Bohemicae ad Anglicanam Paraenesis* (Amsterdam, 1660), Dedication to the Church of England, paras 19-20.

Reformed court chaplain in Berlin (from 1693) and a bishop of the *Unitas Fratrum* (from 1699), Jablonski corresponded between 1695 and 1713 with a number of Anglican clergymen and bishops about various matters including protestant union and Continental protestant concerns. Latterly, his correspondents included three Tory high-churchmen – Archbishop Sharp of York, Bishop John Robinson (then of Bristol), and George Smalridge (later bishop of Bristol). Jablonski visited London in 1709, becoming a corresponding member of the SPCK.

In 1683 a letter from Adam Samuel Hartmann to his brother Paul had resulted in a royal 'brief' encouraging a collection for the Bohemian Brethren, who continued to suffer in Poland, but it was a fresh appeal for financial assistance in 1716 (Lissa having again been burnt in 1706) which made the Bohemian Brethren the subject of public discussion in England. Christian Sitkovius (later Jablonski's fellow-bishop) was sent as a delegate, and Archbishop Wake secured an Order in Council encouraging collections on their behalf. Hearing that the *Unitas Fratrum's* episcopal succession had been questioned by some (although defended by others), Jablonski wrote to Wake, putting the Brethren's case. In his reply, Wake accepted the validity of the Bohemian succession. Their correspondence continued until 1732.

The Moravian Church

Representatives of the Herrnhut community visited England in 1728 (to seek fellowship with Christians in England) and 1735 (*en route* for Britain's American colonies). In 1735 David Nitschmann was consecrated a bishop of the *Unitas Fratrum* in the hope that the orders of missionaries ordained by him would be recognized in British colonies, and in 1737 Count Zinzendorf came to London with Nitschmann to seek Anglican advice as to whether he should himself accept consecration as a bishop. Archbishop Potter, who knew of the *Unitas Fratrum's* traditions and accepted its succession, told Zinzendorf that this was a God-given opportunity to renew and conserve an episcopal church for which God still had plans, and should not be allowed to pass. The Moravian Church, he told the count, was closer to the Church of England than any other; the

Moravians were 'our brethren, and one Church with our own'.[5] In 1739 a Moravian envoy was sent to another high-church Anglican bishop, the saintly Thomas Wilson of Sodor and Man. To both bishops the Moravian episcopal succession was important, as was their orthodoxy. Another important factor for their appreciation of the Moravian Church was its 'apostolicity'. Potter regarded its bishops, such as the carpenter Nitschmann, as very similar to those of the primitive Church, and both Potter and Wilson saw in it the doctrine and discipline of the primitive Church preserved, Wilson describing the Moravian discipline as 'certainly the best' and 'nearest to that of the Primitive Church'. For Wilson the *Unitas Fratrum*'s persecution by Roman Catholicism was significant, and above all he admired the Moravians' missionary endeavours.

The establishment of the first Moravian congregations in England, for Yorkshire (May 1742) and London (October 1742) created a new situation. In June and October Moravian ministers called on Archbishop Potter to explain that despite these developments they did not wish to be regarded as dissenters. However, the registration of the Moravians' Fetter Lane Chapel in London under the Toleration Act that September did imply dissent from the Church of England. The Moravians' English followers were divided; some wished fervently to remain within the Church of England, while others were very critical of the prevailing situation within the Established Church and content to accept separation from it. When the Moravian ministers called on him, the Archbishop again spoke of the Moravian and Anglican Churches as 'sister churches', but warned that Anglicans should not be received into the Moravian Church in significant numbers.

Admiration for the Moravian Church was not universal amongst Anglican bishops, however. In 1744 Bishop Gibson, in whose diocese of London one of the two congregations was situated (and who in 1735 had been the first Anglican bishop to receive a Moravian visitor) attacked the Moravians in an anonymous tract. When Moravian delegates visited him to seek a rapprochement, he referred to the Anglican and Moravian Churches as 'sister churches' only to make his point that it was 'not fair'

---

[5] For the period 1735-1750, see C.J. Podmore, 'The Bishops and the Brethren: Anglican Attitudes to the Moravians in the Mid-Eighteenth Century', *Journal of Ecclesiastical History*, xli (1990), 622-46.

for one church to seek to introduce its discipline into another church; such conduct was 'not the way to cultivate a good correspondence between the churches'. Thereafter he refused to receive Moravian visitors, complaining at 'Bishops and Presbyters breaking in upon the fixed Provinces or Bounds of one another'.

Zinzendorf, a passionate worker for Christian unity credited with being the first to use the word *oikoumene* in its modern sense (as describing the whole Christian Church in its varied manifestations), struggled throughout the 1740s to reconcile the existence of the Moravian Church in England with his ecumenical ideals. In 1746 he came to England to propose to Archbishop Potter a plan to enable those who joined the Moravian Church to enjoy Moravian worship and discipline without thereby separating from the Church of England. Effectively, the proposals added up to the organization of Anglicans received into the Moravian Church as a non-parochial society under the general oversight of an Anglican bishop (Zinzendorf suggested Potter himself, acting in a personal capacity). Moravians who preached publicly in England would be ordained by an Anglican bishop, and an Anglican bishop would be invited to assist in any Moravian consecration taking place in England. John Gambold, an Anglican priest (ordained by Potter) who had become a Moravian, would be appointed one of Potter's chaplains. Archbishop Potter replied that in the absence of a formal recognition by the Church of England of the *Unitas Fratrum's* episcopate, an Anglican bishop was unlikely to participate in a Moravian consecration, and even if one did, the Anglican ordinal would have to be used. Furthermore, Zinzendorf's scheme could not even be discussed without authority from the Privy Council. At the time, Zinzendorf's proposals were unrealistic, but a century later (when government supervision of the Church of England was diminished) the development of the Anglican religious orders was to demonstrate that the Anglican system could be adapted to provide for extra-parochial societies.

The failure of Zinzendorf's scheme meant that the Church of England and the Moravian Church in England would be two separate churches; the most that could be hoped for was official recognition of the Moravian episcopate. This was achieved in 1749, when an act of Parliament describing the Moravian Church as 'an antient Protestant Episcopal Church' was obtained. Before the Moravian bill came before the House of

Lords, the Anglican bench of bishops met at Lambeth Palace and decided to support it. In the meantime, Gibson had died, as had the increasingly cautious Potter, who was succeeded by Thomas Herring, a strong advocate of toleration. Instrumental in the bishops' decision was the Bishop of Lincoln, John Thomas. In a speech in the House of Lords the previous year, opposing the Bill for Disarming the Scottish Highlands (which banned Scottish episcopalian clergy not ordained by bishops of the Churches of England or Ireland), he argued that true bishops did not have to be like those of the English and Irish established churches. His example was the bishops of the *Unitas Fratrum*, who, he said, were not lords, had no geographical dioceses, no involvement in public affairs and no revenues, indeed sometimes worked with their hands like the apostles, but were still valid bishops with a succession as good as, if not better than, that of the Church of England. When the Moravian bill reached its committee stage the Anglican bishops turned out in force to support it, seventeen of the twenty-six attending one or both of the sessions. The attendance of fifteen at the first was almost double the average, and greater than that for two of the three previous bills in the past fifteen years on which the bishops had taken a distinctive corporate line. The bill was steered through the Lords by Bishop Maddox of Worcester.

The following eighteen months were the high point of relations between the Moravian Church and the Anglican episcopate. Bishop Sherlock of London visited Zinzendorf, while the Bishop of Lincoln invited the count to his palace. Both showed surprising appreciation of Zinzendorf's otherwise controversial theological language, and there was general agreement on doctrinal matters. Contact with these and other bishops continued in 1750 and subsequent years. In 1750 Bishop Wilson even accepted the honorary presidency of the Moravian General Synod.

Public approbation of the Moravians was, however, severely dented by the publication in 1753 of Henry Rimius' *Candid Narrative of the Rise and Progress of the Herrnhuters*, the first of a series of publications in which Rimius attacked the Moravian Church, making use of Continental anti-Moravian literature.[7] Rimius later claimed that he began his campaign against the Moravian Church at Archbishop Herring's request, and there

---

[7] For the period 1750-1763, see C.J. Podmore, 'The Role of the Moravian Church in England: 1728-1760', ch. IX.

is some evidence to support this. The publication was certainly approved by the Archbishop, to whom it was dedicated 'by permission', and from at least the end of 1753 he directed Rimius' campaign. In December 1754 Bishop Lavington of Exeter, who had previously included attacks on the Moravians in *The Enthusiasm of Methodists and Papists Compared* (1749-51), joined the fray with *The Moravians Compared and Detected*. Thereafter, at Herring's request, Lavington took over detailed direction of the campaign. By 1755 Rimius' revelations had turned the Anglican episcopate against the Moravians. When his financial affairs reached a crisis at the end of 1755 and Herring organized a collection to pay his debts, the subscribers included both archbishops, the Bishop of London and nine other Anglican bishops. Only Maddox remained loyal to the Moravians, assisting with the composition of tracts they published in their defence.

The Anglican bishops' attitude to Moravian orders was tested in 1763, when Lord Dartmouth offered the curacy of Olney in Buckinghamshire to Francis Okely. Okely applied to the Bishop of Lincoln, John Green, for ordination to the priesthood, supplying evidence of his Moravian ordination to the diaconate in 1747. The Bishop consulted Archbishop Secker, who advised rejection and included Okely's name in a letter warning the Bishop of Rochester about men who were not to be ordained or recognized as clergy. Secker's decision seems to have been based on objection to Moravian teachings and practices, as represented in the anti-Moravian tracts of the 1750s, and an unwillingness to countenance them within the Church of England. The doubt which he expressed about Moravian orders and the difficulty of obtaining documentation of Moravian ordinations seem more like attempts to justify his stance than reasons for it. The Bishop of Lincoln's reply to Okely gave three reasons why his ordination to the diaconate could not be recognized: the preamble to the 1749 act describing the Moravian Church as episcopal had been drawn up hastily from the Moravians' own claims and was in no way binding on the Church of England; the historical account of the Moravians' episcopal succession was obscure and disputed; and there existed neither an established channel of communication with the Moravian Church, nor criteria for deciding which of its ministers were bishops whose orders were accepted by the Church of England, nor any way of ascertaining 'how their Orders are genuine'. Bishops gathered for the monthly meeting of Queen Anne's Bounty in December 1763 advised Green not to ordain

Okely to the priesthood, but postponed a definite decision on Moravian orders to a later, fuller meeting of the episcopate. This Okely forestalled by withdrawing his application. Green's mind was made up, however. Okely was added to the list of those 'not to be permitted to serve Cures within the Diocese of Lincoln' on the grounds that he was 'not in Orders'.

In 1769 the Moravian Church secured a grant of land on the Labrador coast as a centre for a mission to Labrador, and fourteen missionaries sailed in 1771. This renewed missionary activity greatly increased the Moravians' standing in London and won them renewed respect. The London Association in Aid of the Missions of the United Brethren was established in 1817 to enable members of other churches, including the Church of England, to support Moravian missionary work, and many Anglican clergy and parishes did so.

From the 1830s, the Oxford Movement fostered increased awareness on the part of Anglicans of their place as part of the wider Catholic Church. This encouraged ecumenical endeavour in some directions, but also focused attention on the existence or otherwise of an unbroken episcopal succession in other churches. In an article published in the *British Magazine* in 1836 and republished, with additions, as a tract in 1841, the Hon. and Revd A.P. Perceval, a chaplain to the Queen, examined the Moravians' 'claim to the possession of the apostolic commission, which they assert has legitimately descended to them, by episcopal succession', but concluded that such claims 'are not so supported, as to entitle [the Moravians] to recognition by the Catholic Church'.[8]

---

[8] A.P. Perceval, 'On the Episcopacy of the Moravians' (reprinted as Chapter IX of A.P. Perceval, *A Collection of Papers connected with the Theological Movement of 1833* (London, 1842)), pp.78, 89.

The Modern Anglican-Moravian Conversations

The modern Anglican-Moravian conversations were among the earliest fostered by the Lambeth Conferences, and like many modern ecumenical endeavours, they can be traced back to the needs of the Church in the mission field.[9] Bishop Mitchinson of Barbados asked at the 1878 Lambeth Conference whether Anglican bishops could commission Moravian bishops to ordain or confirm on their behalf (and *vice versa*), whether Anglican and Moravian ministers could officiate in each other's churches, and whether a Moravian minister wishing to enter the Anglican ministry should be (re-)ordained, conditionally ordained or simply received. The questions were referred to a committee, but no report was produced.

Following a repeated request from the West Indies, the 1888 Conference established a committee, which requested information about the origins of Moravian episcopacy from the Unity Elders Conference in Herrnhut, which in turn commissioned a report from the Unity Archivist, Joseph Theodor Müller. His report, published in 1889, pointed to two gaps in the Moravian succession (in 1500 and 1553), but the UEC's reply to the Anglican committee took a much more positive view. As one of the committee members, Bishop Stubbs of Oxford, declined to sign the report, it remained a draft, and the 1897 Lambeth Conference therefore declined to consider it, instead requesting the appointment of a further committee. Both of these Lambeth Conferences praised the Moravians' work and approach in the mission field, and the 1897 Conference considered that it was 'obviously a matter of expediency as well as of duty to bridge over or remove the obstacles which at present separate the two communions'.

At the beginning of the twentieth century the focus switched to England. In 1901 a Moravian minister expressed a desire to serve as a minister of the Church of England; Archbishop Benson therefore commissioned a study, which indicated that Moravian orders had never been recognized by the Church of England. In 1902 the Moravian Church established a committee to enquire into the possibility of closer Anglican-Moravian

---

[9] For the period 1878-1991, see C.J. Podmore, 'Anglican-Moravian Dialogue since 1878', *One in Christ*, xxvii (1991), 150-165.

relations. These developments culminated in the appointment by the Archbishop of a 'Committee. . . to consider the Orders of the *Unitas Fratrum* or Moravians'. Its conclusion that the unbroken Moravian episcopal succession dated only from 1553 laid to rest hopes of Anglican recognition of Moravian orders.

The Anglican desire for communion with the Moravian Church remained unabated, however, and the 1908 Lambeth Conference, which again praised the Moravian Church's 'noble record of missionary service', therefore proposed a scheme for the gradual establishment of an interchangeable ministry by Anglican participation in Moravian consecrations. Conditions were attached, however, which reflected an increased concern for visible unity and the avoidance of parallel jurisdictions. Anglicans were increasingly unwilling to establish interchangeability of ministries without setting this within a wider reconciliation of the churches. Negotiations began with the British Province of the Moravian Church, but full agreement was not reached. After a request from the 1920 Lambeth Conference, the Moravian committee agreed to recommend restriction of celebration of the Eucharist to presbyters. It would also recommend that a commission to confirm should be given to presbyters at their ordination, but its response to the other conditions set by the 1908 Lambeth Conference was firmer. The Lambeth Conference had insisted that the Moravians should explain their position 'as that of a religious community or missionary body in close alliance with the Anglican Church' and give 'due recognition to the position of [Anglican] Bishops within Anglican Dioceses and jurisdictions'. The Moravian Committee now responded that the only basis for co-operation would be 'the full mutual recognition of two independent Churches, working together on lines agreeable to both'. Discussions continued until 1923, but failed to reach agreement.

The 1930 Lambeth Conference re-affirmed Anglican admiration for Moravian missionary work. By now, the London Association included five English diocesan bishops and other senior Anglican clergy among its vice-presidents. The Lambeth Conference, stressing the importance of Anglican-Moravian relations in the mission field and reflecting on the fact that discussions had continued for over forty years, appointed a new committee to confer with a committee of the Moravian Church, with a view to a final decision at the next Lambeth Conference. In 1936 the

Anglican committee reported that an agreed basis for steps towards intercommunion could not be found. The 1948 Lambeth Conference accepted the end of specific Anglican-Moravian conversations, and expressed instead the hope that progress would be made through general Anglican conversations with the Free Churches.

These conversations culminated in 1982 in the proposed Covenant for Unity between the Church of England, the Moravian Church, the Methodist Church and the United Reformed Church. The General Synod of the Church of England was unable to endorse the Covenant, but the Moravian Church's Provincial Synod nevertheless went on to approve it by a vote of 98% in favour.

In 1984 the Moravian Synod authorized the Provincial Board and the Faith and Order Committee to examine the possibility of further moves towards unity with other churches and to enter into discussion with them if this seemed desirable. The Committee decided that it would be appropriate to approach the Church of England, and did so in February 1985. After an initial exploratory meeting, the General Synod's Standing Committee agreed to formal Conversations, which began in 1989 and concluded in 1995.

Appendices

CONTENTS

	Page
The Canberra Statement: The Unity of the Church as Koinonia: Gift and Calling	85
The Office of Bishop in our Churches: Texts	88
The International Structures of our Churches	97
Anglican Dioceses and Moravian Congregations in England	101
Provinces of the Moravian Church and Churches of the Anglican Communion	104

THE CANBERRA STATEMENT

THE UNITY OF THE CHURCH AS KOINONIA: GIFT AND CALLING*

1.1 The purpose of God according to holy scripture is to gather the whole of creation under the Lordship of Christ Jesus in whom, by the power of the Holy Spirit, all are brought into communion with God (Eph. 1). The church is the foretaste of this communion with God and with one another. The grace of our Lord Jesus Christ, the love of God, and the communion of the Holy Spirit enable the one church to live as sign of the reign of God and servant of the reconciliation with God, promised and provided for the whole creation. The purpose of the church is to unite people with Christ in the power of the Spirit, to manifest communion in prayer and action and thus to point to the fullness of communion with God, humanity and the whole creation in the glory of the kingdom.

1.2 The calling of the church is to proclaim reconciliation and provide healing, to overcome divisions based on race, gender, age, culture, colour, and to bring all people into communion with God. Because of sin and the misunderstanding of the diverse gifts of the Spirit, the churches are painfully divided within themselves and among each other. The scandalous divisions damage the credibility of their witness to the world in worship and service. Moreover they contradict not only the church's witness but also its very nature.

1.3 We acknowledge with gratitude to God that in the ecumenical movement the churches walk together in mutual understanding, theological convergence, common suffering and common prayer, shared witness and service as they draw close to one another. This has allowed them to recognize a certain degree of communion already existing between them. This is indeed the fruit of the active presence of the Holy Spirit in the midst of all who believe in Christ Jesus and who struggle for visible unity now. Nevertheless churches have failed to draw the consequences for their

---

* This statement was adapted by the Seventh Assembly of the World Council of Churches in Canberra in February 1991. It was published in *Signs of the Spirit, Official Report, WCC Seventh Assembly*, ed. M. Kinnamon (Geneva, 1991), pp. 172ff.

life from the degree of communion they have already experienced and the agreements already achieved. They have remained satisfied to co-exist in division.

2.1 The unity of the church to which we are called is a koinonia given and expressed in the common confession of the apostolic faith; a common sacramental life entered by the one baptism and celebrated together in one eucharist fellowship; a common life in which members and ministries are mutually recognized and reconciled; and a common mission witnessing to the gospel of God's grace to all people and serving the whole of creation. The goal of the search for full communion is realized when all the churches are able to recognize in one another the one, holy, catholic and apostolic church in its fullness. This full communion will be expressed on the local and the universal levels through conciliar forms of life and action. In such communion churches are bound in all aspects of their life together at all levels in confessing the one faith and engaging in worship and witness, deliberation and action.

2.2 Diversities which are rooted in theological traditions, various cultural, ethnic or historical contacts are integral to the nature of communion; yet there are limits to diversity. Diversity is illegitimate when, for instance, it makes impossible the common confession of Jesus Christ as God and Saviour the same yesterday, today and forever (Heb. 13.8); and salvation and the final destiny of humanity as proclaimed in holy scripture and preached by the apostolic community. In communion diversities are brought together in harmony as gifts of the Holy Spirit, contributing to the richness and fullness of the church of God.

3.1 Many things have been done and many remain to be done on the way towards the realization of full communion. Churches have reached agreements in bilateral and multilateral dialogues which are already bearing fruit, renewing their liturgical and spiritual life and their theology. In taking specific steps together the churches express and encourage the enrichment and renewal of Christian life, as they learn from one another, work together for justice and peace, and care together for God's creation.

3.2 The challenge at this moment in the ecumenical movement as a reconciling and renewing movement towards full visible unity is for the seventh assembly of the WCC to call all churches:

- to recognize each other's baptism on the basis of the BEM document;
- to move towards the recognition of the apostolic faith as expressed through the Nicene-Constantinopolitan Creed in the life and witness of one another;
- on the basis of convergence in faith in baptism, eucharist and ministry to consider, wherever appropriate, forms of eucharistic hospitality; we gladly acknowledge that some who do not observe these rites share in the spiritual experience of life in Christ;
- to move towards a mutual recognition of ministries;
- to endeavour in word and deed to give common witness to the gospel as a whole;
- to recommit themselves to work for justice, peace and the integrity of creation, linking more closely the search for the sacramental communion of the church with the struggle for justice and peace;
- to help parishes and communities express in appropriate ways locally the degree of communion that already exists.

4.1 The Holy Spirit as promoter of koinonia (2 Cor. 13.13) gives to those who are still divided the thirst and hunger for full communion. We remain restless until we grow together according to the wish and prayer of Christ that those who believe in him may be one (John 17.21). In the process of praying, working and struggling for unity, the Holy Spirit comforts us in pain, disturbs us when we are satisfied to remain in our divisions, leads us to repentance, and grants us joy when our communion flourishes.

THE OFFICE OF BISHOP IN OUR CHURCHES: TEXTS

A THE MORAVIAN CHURCH

1. Extracts from *The Church Order of the Unitas Fratrum (Moravian Church), 1988*

104(a) The Unitas Fratrum recognises the priesthood of all believers but also has specially appointed ministers who receive commission and authority for their service from the hands of Jesus Christ, Whom the Church acknowledges as its Chief Elder. All members may gladly and confidently carry on their work in and for the congregation and by their devotion and faithfulness all can render service to the whole Church.

(b) At the same time the Unitas Fratrum gratefully acknowledges the gift of the offices of the ministry which it has received from the Lord. It recognises and confesses that in reality it is its Lord and Head Jesus Christ Who calls and ordains, whether in the case of the reception as an acolyte or the ordination to the office of Deacon, or the consecration as a Presbyter or Bishop.

(c) The same is true for the brethren and sisters who are called or elected to service in any official capacity. They can render their service well only through the grace of their Chief Elder.

Ordination in General

682. The constituted orders of the ministry in the Moravian Church are those of Deacons, Presbyters and Bishops. Those who are ordained are authorised to administer the Sacraments in the Moravian Church.

683. Only the Provincial Board, the Provincial or Unity Synod has the authority to commission ordination. In extending such a commission they are guided by careful consideration of the spiritual, mental and physical qualifications of the candidate for ordination. The Board also designates the bishop who is to officiate in this act. Ordination should be preceded by appropriate ministerial training (cf. para. 692).

684. The ordained Minister remains a servant of Christ and the Church as a whole, not merely of the congregation to which he/she is called. Even as Jesus Christ came not to be ministered unto but to minister, so His servants should be willing to minister wherever the Church calls them under the leading of the Holy Spirit.

The Office of a Bishop

687. The Renewed Unity received the episcopacy as an inheritance from the Ancient Unitas Fratrum.

Today we regard the episcopacy in the Renewed Unity in a different way from that of the Ancient Unitas Fratrum. Formerly, a Bishop had a Church-governmental and administrative function. In our day, this function is not necessarily linked to the episcopal office.

A Bishop of the Moravian Church is consecrated to a special priestly-pastoral ministry in the name of and for the whole Unity.

A Bishop is a living symbol of the continuity of the Church's Ministry, although the Unity does not place emphasis on any mechanical transmission of the apostolic succession.

The office and function of a Bishop is valid throughout the Unity as a whole.

Duties of Bishops

688. A Bishop as a Bishop primarily has spiritual responsibility in the Church. The Synod of his Province may add administrative responsibility by electing him a member of the Provincial Board.

All Provincial and district Boards shall consult a Bishop or Bishops in all matters concerning the work in the Province or District which fall within his sphere of responsibility.

A Bishop has a special duty of intercession for the Unity, and also for the Church of Christ as a whole.

A Bishop is a pastor to pastors.

Bishops in active service should be enabled to visit Congregations for the deepening of their spiritual life.

The opinion of a Bishop (Bishops) shall customarily be sought and given due consideration and weight in matters of doctrine and practice.

A Bishop represents the Church in the act of Ordination.

A Bishop alone has the right to consecrate to the various orders of the Ministry, but only when he is commissioned to do so by the Provincial Board or Synod of a Unity Province.

A Bishop, however, has the right to decline a commission to ordain, should he wish to do so.

In exceptional cases the ordination of a Deacon may be performed by a Presbyter in the name of and by commission of a Bishop.

A Bishop (Bishops) should share in the decisions regarding the training of candidates for the ministry and should maintain a special pastoral relationship with such candidates throughout their training.

Election of Bishops

689. Wherever possible, at least one Bishop should be resident in every Province.

A Bishop is not appointed by any Provincial Board, but shall be elected from among the Presbyters either by a Provincial Synod, or in a Provincial Election ordered by the Synod under regulations contained in its constitution.

The election of a Bishop in an Affiliated Province shall be carried out under the regulations laid down by the Synod of the Province to which it is related.

On the occasion of the consecration of a Bishop, at least two Bishops of the Unity must officiate.

690. All Provinces entitled under the Constitution of the Unitas Fratrum to elect and consecrate Bishops shall, on the occasion of the consecration of a Bishop, send to the Chairman of the Unity Board notification of such consecration, giving the name of the brother so consecrated, the names of the officiating Bishops and the date and place of the consecration, and the Chairman of the Unity Board shall transmit this information to all Provinces of the Unity and to the Archivist at Herrnhut.

2. Extract from *The Moravian Liturgy, authorised for use in the British Province of the Moravian Church (Unitas Fratrum)*, (1960): The Ordination of Ministers

Prayer at the Consecration of a Bishop

Almighty and most merciful Father, we thank thee that of thine infinite goodness thou hast given thine only and dearly beloved son, Jesus Christ, to be our Redeemer, and the Author of everlasting life; who after that he had made perfect our redemption by his death, and was ascended into heaven, poured down his gifts abundantly upon men, making some, apostles; some, prophets; some, evangelists; some, pastors and teachers; to the edifying and making perfect his Church: grant, we beseech thee, to this thy servant such grace that he may evermore be ready to spread abroad thy Gospel, the glad tidings of reconciliation with thee; so that, as a wise and faithful servant, giving to thy family their portion in due season, he may at last be received into everlasting joy; through Jesus Christ our Lord, who with thee and the Holy Ghost liveth and reigneth, one God, world without end. AMEN.

The Candidates kneel, and with the Laying on of Hands by the Bishops present, the Presiding Bishop says:

M.M. I *ordain* (consecrate) thee to be a *Deacon* (Presbyter) (Bishop) in the Church of God, in the name of the Father, and of the Son, and of the Holy Ghost. AMEN.

> The Lord bless thee, and keep thee;
>> The Lord make his face to shine upon thee,
>> and be gracious unto thee;
>
> The Lord lift up his countenance upon thee,
>> and give thee peace.
>>> *In the name of Jesus.* AMEN.

B THE CHURCH OF ENGLAND

1. Canons of the Church of England

C 1 OF HOLY ORDERS IN THE CHURCH OF ENGLAND

1. The Church of England holds and teaches that from the Apostles' time there have been these orders in Christ's Church: bishops, priests, and deacons; and no man shall be accounted or taken to be a lawful bishop, priest, or deacon in the Church of England, or suffered to execute any of the said offices, except he be called, tried, examined, and admitted thereunto according to the Ordinal or any form of service alternative thereto approved by the General Synod under Canon B 2, authorised by the Archbishops of Canterbury and York under Canon C 4A or has had formerly episcopal consecration or ordination in some Church whose orders are recognised and accepted by the Church of England.

2. No person who has been admitted to the order of bishop, priest, or deacon can ever be divested of the character of his order, but a minister may either by legal process voluntarily relinquish the exercise of his orders and use himself as a layman, or may by legal and canonical process be deprived of the exercise of his orders or deposed finally therefrom.

3. According to the ancient law and usage of this Church and Realm of England, the inferior clergy who have received authority to minister in any diocese owe canonical obedience in all things lawful and honest to the bishop of the same, and the bishop of each diocese owes due allegiance to the archbishop of the province as his metropolitan.

C 2 OF THE CONSECRATION OF BISHOPS

1. No person shall be consecrated to the office of bishop by fewer than three bishops present together and joining in the act of consecration, of whom one shall be the archbishop of the province or a bishop appointed to act on his behalf.

2. The consecration of a bishop shall take place upon some Sunday or Holy Day, unless the archbishop, for urgent and weighty cause, shall appoint some other day.

3. No person shall be consecrated bishop except he shall be at least thirty years of age.

4. No person shall be refused consecration as bishop on the ground that he was born out of wedlock.

C 17 OF ARCHBISHOPS

1. By virtue of their respective offices, the Archbishop of Canterbury is styled Primate of All England and Metropolitan, and the Archbishop of York Primate of England and Metropolitan.

2. The archbishop has throughout his province at all times metropolitical jurisdiction, as superintendent of all ecclesiastical matters therein, to correct and supply the defects of other bishops, and, during the time of his metropolitical visitation, jurisdiction as Ordinary, except in places and over persons exempt by law or custom.

3. Such jurisdiction is exercised by the archbishop himself, or by a vicar-general, official, or other commissary to whom authority in that behalf shall have been formally committed by the archbishop concerned.

4. The archbishop is, within his province, the principal minister, and to him belongs the right of confirming the election of every person to a bishopric, of being the chief consecrator at the consecration of every bishop, of receiving such appeals in his provincial court as may be provided by law, of holding metropolitical visitations at times or places limited by law or custom, and of presiding in the Convocation of the province either in person or by such deputy as he may lawfully appoint. In the province of Canterbury, the Bishop of London or, in his absence, the Bishop of Winchester, has the right to be so appointed; and in their absence the archbishop shall appoint some other diocesan bishop of the province. The two archbishops are joint presidents of the General Synod.

5. By ancient custom, no Act is held to be an Act of the Convocation of the province unless it shall have received the assent of the archbishop.

6. By statute law it belongs to the archbishop to give permission to officiate within his province to any minister who has been ordained priest or deacon by an overseas bishop within the meaning of the Overseas and Other Clergy (Ministry and Ordination) Measure 1967, or a bishop in a Church not in communion with the Church of England whose orders are recognised or accepted by the Church of England, and thereupon such minister shall possess all such rights and advantages and be subject to all such duties and liabilities as he would have possessed and been subject to if he had been ordained by the bishop of a diocese in the province of Canterbury or York.

7. By the laws of this realm the Archbishop of Canterbury is empowered to grant such licences or dispensations as are therein set forth and provided, and such licences or dispensations, being confirmed by the authority of the Queen's Majesty, have force and authority not only within the province of Canterbury but throughout all England.

C 18 OF DIOCESAN BISHOPS

1. Every bishop is the chief pastor of all that are within his diocese, as well laity and clergy, and their father in God; it appertains to his office to teach and to uphold sound and wholesome doctrine, and to banish and drive away all erroneous and strange opinions; and, himself an example of righteous and godly living, it is his duty to set forward and maintain quietness, love, and peace among all men.

2. Every bishop has within his diocese jurisdiction as Ordinary except in places and over persons exempt by law or custom.

3. Such jurisdiction is exercised by the bishop himself, or by a vicar-general, official, or other commissary, to whom authority in that behalf shall have been formally committed by the bishop concerned.

4. Every bishop is, within his diocese, the principal minister, and to him belongs the right, save in places and over persons exempt by law or custom, of celebrating the rites of ordination and confirmation; of conducting, ordering, controlling, and authorising all services in churches, chapels, churchyards and consecrated burial grounds; of granting a faculty or licence for all alterations, additions, removals, or repairs to the walls, fabric, ornaments, or furniture of the same; of consecrating new churches, churchyards, and burial grounds; of instituting to all vacant benefices, whether of his own collation or of the presentation of others; of admitting by licence to all other vacant ecclesiastical offices; of holding visitations at times limited by law or custom to the end that he may get some good knowledge of the state, sufficiency, and ability of the clergy and other persons whom he is to visit; of being president of the diocesan synod.

5. Where the assent of the bishop is required to a resolution of the diocesan synod it shall not lightly nor without grave cause be withheld.

6. Every bishop shall be faithful in admitting persons into holy orders and celebrating the rite of confirmation as often and in as many places as shall be convenient, and shall provide, as much as in him lies, that in every place within his diocese there shall be sufficient priests to minister the word and sacraments to the people that are therein.

7. Every bishop shall correct and punish all such as be unquiet, disobedient, or criminous, within his diocese, according to such authority as he has by God's Word and is committed to him by the laws and ordinances of this realm.

8. Every bishop shall reside within his diocese, saving the ancient right of any bishop, when resident in any house in London during his attendance on the Parliament, or on the Court, or for the purpose of performing any other duties of his office, to be taken and accounted as resident within his own diocese.

C 20 OF BISHOPS SUFFRAGAN

1. Every bishop suffragan shall endeavour himself faithfully to execute such things pertaining to the episcopal office as shall be delegated to him by the bishop of the diocese to whom he shall be suffragan.

2. Every bishop suffragan shall use, have, or execute only such jurisdiction or episcopal power or authority in any diocese as shall be licensed or limited to him to use, have, or execute by the bishop of the same.

3. Every bishop suffragan shall reside within the diocese of the bishop to whom he shall be suffragan, except he have a licence from that bishop to reside elsewhere.

2a. Extract from the Ordinal, 1662: The Form of Ordaining or Consecrating of an Archbishop or Bishop

ALMIGHTY God, and most merciful Father, who of thine infinite goodness hast given thine only and dearly loved Son Jesus Christ, to be our Redeemer, and the Author of everlasting life; who, after that he had made perfect our Redemption by his death, and was ascended into heaven, poured down his gifts abundantly upon men, making some Apostles, some Prophets, some Evangelists, some Pastors and Doctors, to the edifying and making perfect his Church; Grant, we beseech thee, to this thy servant such grace, that he may evermore be ready to spread abroad thy Gospel, the glad tidings of reconciliation with thee; and use the authority given him, not to destruction, but to salvation; not to hurt, but to help: so that as a wise and faithful servant, giving to thy family their portion in due season, he may at last be received into everlasting joy; through Jesus Christ our Lord, who with thee and the Holy Ghost liveth and reigneth, one God, world without end. Amen

Then the Archbishop and Bishops present shall lay their hands upon the head of the elected Bishop kneeling before them upon his knees, the Archbishop saying,

RECEIVE the Holy Ghost, for the Office and Work of a Bishop in the Church of God, now committed unto thee by the Imposition of our hands; In the Name of the Father, and of the Son, and of the Holy Ghost. Amen. And remember that thou stir up the grace of God which is given thee by this Imposition of our hands; for God hath not given us the spirit of fear, but of power, and love and soberness.

Then the Archbishop shall deliver him the Bible, saying,

Give heed unto reading, exhortation and doctrine. Think upon the things contained in this Book. Be diligent in them, that the increase coming thereby may be manifest unto all men. Take heed unto thyself, and to doctrine, and be diligent in doing them: for by so doing thou shalt both save thyself and them that hear thee. Be to the flock of Christ a shepherd, not a wolf; feed them, devour them not. Hold up the weak, heal the sick, bind up the broken, bring again the out-casts, seek the lost. Be so merciful, that you be not too remiss; so minister discipline, that you forget not mercy: that when the chief Shepherd shall appear you may receive the never-fading crown of glory; through Jesus Christ our Lord. *Amen.*

2b. Extract from The Alternative Service Book, 1980: The Ordination or Consecration of a Bishop

THE DECLARATION

13 *The Bishop-elect stands before the Archbishop, and the people sit.*

Archbishop

A Bishop is called to lead in serving and caring for the people of God and to work with them in the oversight of the Church. As a chief pastor he shares with his fellow bishops a special responsibility to maintain and further the unity of the Church, to uphold its discipline, and to guard its faith. He is to promote its mission throughout the world. It is his duty to watch over and pray for all those committed to his charge, and to teach and govern them after the example of the Apostles, speaking in the name of God and interpreting the gospel of Christ. He is to know his people and be known by them. He is to ordain and to send new ministers, guiding those who serve with him and enabling them to fulfil their ministry.

He is to baptize and confirm, to preside at the Holy Communion, and to lead the offering of prayer and praise. He is to be merciful, but with firmness, and to minister discipline, but with mercy. He is to have a special care for the outcast and needy; and to those who turn to God he is to declare the forgiveness of sins.

THE ORDINATION

18 *The Archbishop stands with the bishops who assist him; the Bishop-elect kneels before him; he stretches out his hands towards him, and says*

19 We praise and glorify you, almighty Father, because you have formed throughout the world a holy people for your own possession, a royal priesthood, a universal Church.

We praise and glorify you because you have given us your only Son Jesus Christ to be the Apostle and High Priest of our faith, and the Shepherd of our souls.

We praise and glorify you that by his death he has overcome death; and that, having ascended into heaven, he has given his gifts abundantly to your people, making some, apostles; some, prophets; some, evangelists; some, pastors and teachers; to equip them for the work of ministry and to build up his body.

An now we give you thanks that you have called this your servant, whom we consecrate in your name, to share this ministry entrusted to your Church.

Here the Archbishop and other bishops lay their hands on the head of the Bishop-elect, and the Archbishop says

Send down the Holy Spirit upon your servant N for the office and work of a bishop in your Church.

The Archbishop then continues

Almighty Father, fill this your servant with the grace and power which you gave to your apostles, that he may lead those committed to his charge in proclaiming the gospel of salvation. Through him increase your Church, renew its ministry, and unite its members in a holy fellowship of truth and love. Enable him as a true shepherd to feed and govern your flock; make him wise as a teacher, and steadfast as a guardian of its faith and sacraments. Guide and direct him in presiding at the worship of your people. Give him humility, that he may use his authority to heal, not to hurt; to build up, not to destroy. Defend him from all evil, that as a ruler over your household and an ambassador for Christ he may stand before you blameless, and finally, with all your servants, enter your eternal joy.

Accept our prayers, most merciful Father, through your Son Jesus Christ our Lord, to whom, with you and your Holy Spirit, belong glory and honour, worship and praise, now and for ever. **Amen.**

THE INTERNATIONAL STRUCTURES OF OUR CHURCHES

THE MORAVIAN CHURCH

Unity Synod

Unity Synod, meeting every seven years, shapes the identity and regulates the ongoing life and work of the Moravian Church worldwide. It is the final authority in matters of faith and order. In practice, however, its decisions are often non-directive (e.g. Unity Synod of 1988 authorised the admission of children to Holy Communion prior to Confirmation but left it to each province to decide if this would be appropriate in its own situation). It co-ordinates support for developing provinces and authorises the creation of new provinces.

The decisions of Unity Synod are incorporated into 'Church Order of the Unitas Fratrum'.

Each province appoints delegates to represent it at Unity Synod, in most cases three, of whom two are elected by the Provincial Synod and one is appointed by the Provincial Board. Bishops are not ex-officio members.

Unity Undertakings

These are areas of service or outreach which are the responsibility of the whole Unity, although in practice oversight is delegated to a particular province.

Provinces

The province is the main administrative unit within the Moravian Unity. Typically its boundaries coincide with a national boundary, although there are exceptions, e.g. the Continental Province, which includes congregations in Germany, Holland, Denmark, Sweden and Switzerland, and the four provinces which exist within the state of Tanzania.

The life of a province is normally governed by a Provincial Synod, meeting annually or bienially, at which all congregations within the province are represented. It elects a Provincial Board and other officials, including bishops, as appropriate. It regulates the life of the province within the guidelines and principles laid down by Unity Synod.

Regional Conferences

The four regional conferences are consultative bodies comprising representatives of provinces within a geographical area. They meet periodically to discuss matters of common concern.

Unity Board

This is the standing council of the worldwide Moravian Church from one Unity Synod to the next. It consists of one member of the Provincial Board of each of the provinces governed by a synod. Much of its work is carried out by correspondence.

Its function is to facilitate the development and the unity of the worldwide Moravian Church and to carry out specific tasks assigned to it by Unity Synod, to which it is answerable.

Unity Chairman/Executive

The Chairman is the executive of the Unity Board, assisted by a Vice-Chairman and Executive Committee drawn from the Unity Board in such a way as to be representative of the four Regional Conferences.

THE ANGLICAN COMMUNION

The Anglican Communion has no written overall church order or canons, but is united by four main instruments of unity or 'bonds of communion'.

The Archbishop of Canterbury

The Archbishop of Canterbury is the personal focus of unity for the Anglican Communion, over which he presides. He has no jurisdiction over the autonomous member churches of the Communion, but many of them look to him and his staff at Lambeth Palace for advice and support.

The Lambeth Conference

The Lambeth Conference is a gathering of bishops whose churches are in communion with the See of Canterbury. It meets every ten years at the invitation and under the presidency of the Archbishop of Canterbury. Although the Conference's resolutions have no canonical status and are not binding on the member churches, they do possess a significant degree of moral authority by virtue of the bishops being gathered together. The first Lambeth Conference was held in 1867, and the thirteenth will be held in Canterbury in 1998.

The Anglican Consultative Council

The Anglican Consultative Council, established in 1969, is an international assembly of the Anglican Communion, consisting of bishops, clergy and lay people from each of the member churches. It meets every two or three years. As its name suggests, it is a consultative body, with no legislative powers.

The Primates' Meeting

Since 1979 a meeting of Anglican primates has been held every two or three years. Each member church of the Anglican Communion is represented by its senior primate, archbishop or presiding bishop. The Primates' Meeting facilitates consultation, but cannot take binding decisions.

The Anglican Communion Secretariat

These bodies are serviced by a permanent Secretariat led by the Secretary General of the Anglican Communion. The offices of the Secretariat are in London.

Member Churches

The Anglican Communion includes 32 autonomous member churches, consisting of one or more Provinces. The four United Churches which incorporate former Anglican dioceses are also members, as are six extra-provincial dioceses (five of which have the Archbishop of Canterbury as their Metropolitan).

Each of the churches has its own constitution. All have an episcopal and synodical polity, but it is impossible to generalize more than this. For example, the senior bishop of some churches is merely a *primus inter pares*, whereas other Anglican churches (such as the Church of England) have a primate or primates with metropolitical jurisdiction throughout their respective provinces.

Churches in Communion

In addition to the member churches of the Anglican Communion, there are other churches which are in communion with the See of Canterbury. These include, for example, the Old Catholic churches and most of the Nordic and Baltic Lutheran churches.

ANGLICAN DIOCESES AND MORAVIAN CONGREGATIONS IN ENGLAND

Diocese   *Congregation*

[Anglican Province of Canterbury]
[Moravian Eastern District]

Diocese	Congregation	
Birmingham	Sparkhill United Church, Birmingham	(United: Moravian-URC)
Chelmsford	Harold Road, London E13	
Coventry	Priors Marston	
Derby	Ockbrook	
Leicester	Leicester	(services in Wesley Hall Methodist Church: monthly united service)
London	Fetter Lane Congregation, Chelsea	
	St Margaret's and St George's, Harlesden	(United: Moravian-URC)
	Hornsey – Stoke Newington Society	
Peterborough	Eydon Woodford Halse	
St Albans	St Luke's, Bedford Queen's Park, Bedford	(United: Moravian-URC)

[Moravian Western District]

Bath and Wells	Coronation Avenue, Bath Weston, Bath	
Bristol	Kingswood United Church Malmesbury	(United: Moravian-URC) (LEP (Local Covenant): Anglican, Roman Catholic, Methodist, URC, Friends, Pentecostal)
	Swindon (East) Tytherton	

Gloucester	Brockweir – Chepstow Society
Hereford	Leominster

[Anglican Province of York]
[Moravian Yorkshire District]

Bradford	Baildon Horton Lower Wyke Fulneck, Pudsey
Ripon	– Leeds Society
Wakefield	Gomersal, Cleckheaton Wellhouse, Mirfield

[Moravian Lancashire District]

Chester	Dukinfield
Manchester	Fairfield, Droylsden Wheler Street, Higher Openshaw – Moss Side Society (services at Whalley Range Methodist Church) Salem, Oldham Westwood, Oldham

N.B. *The Moravian Church in Great Britain and Ireland also includes an Irish District, with the following congregations:*

> Cliftonville, Belfast
> University Road, Belfast
> (Lower) Ballinderry, Lisburn, Co. Antrim
> Gracehill, Ballymena, Co. Antrim
> Kilwarlin, Hillsborough, Co. Down

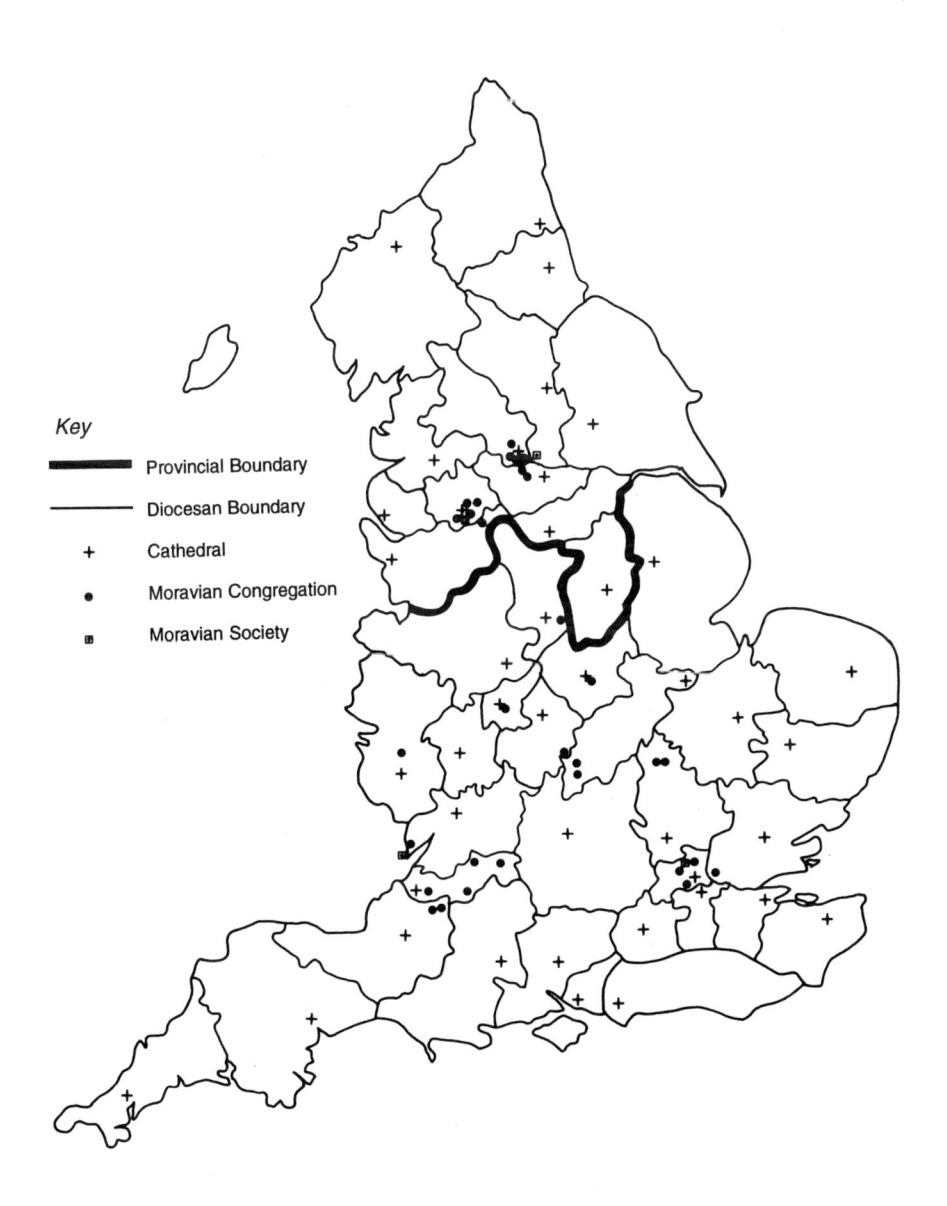

ANGLICAN DIOCESES AND
MORAVIAN CONGREGATIONS IN ENGLAND

PROVINCES OF THE MORAVIAN CHURCH AND CHURCHES OF THE ANGLICAN COMMUNION

PROVINCES OF THE MORAVIAN CHURCH
Alaska
America (North)
America (South)
Britain
Continental European
Czech Republic
Costa Rica
Eastern West Indies
Guyana
Honduras
Jamaica
Labrador
Nicaragua
South Africa
Surinam
Tanzania (Rukwa)
Tanzania (Southern)
Tanzania (South Western)
Tanzania (Western)

Unity Undertakings: North India; Star Mountain, Ramallah

CHURCHES OF THE ANGLICAN COMMUNION
Anglican Church in Aotearoa, New Zealand
Anglican Church of Australia
Episcopal Anglican Church of Brazil
Church of the Province of Burundi
Anglican Church of Canada
Church of the Province of Central Africa
Church of the Province of Southeast Asia
Church of England
Church of the Province of the Indian Ocean
Church of Ireland

Holy Catholic Church in Japan
Episcopal Church in Jerusalem and the Middle East
Church of the Province of Kenya
Anglican Church of Korea
Church of the Province of Melanesia
Anglican Church of Mexico
Church of the Province of Myanmar (Burma)
Church of the Province of Nigeria
Anglican Church of Papua New Guinea
Philippine Episcopal Church
Province of the Episcopal Church of Rwanda
Scottish Episcopal Church
Church of the Province of Southern Africa
Anglican Church of the Southern Cone of America
Episcopal Church of the Sudan
Church of the Province of Tanzania
Church of the Province of Uganda
Episcopal Church in the United States of America [includes Central America, Colombia, Ecuador, Venezuela, Dominican Republic, Puerto Rico]
Church in Wales
Church of the Province of West Africa
Church in the Province of the West Indies
Province of the Anglican Church of Zaire

Extra-provincial churches/dioceses under the metropolitical jurisdiction of the Archbishop of Canterbury:

Anglican Church of Bermuda
Church of Ceylon (Sri Lanka)
Diocese of Hong Kong and Macao
Lusitanian Church of Portugal
Spanish Reformed Episcopal Church

Church under a Metropolitan Council in matters of faith and order:
Episcopal Church of Cuba

United Churches including former Anglican dioceses:
Church of South India
Church of North India
Church of Pakistan
Church of Bangladesh

CORRELATION OF MORAVIAN PROVINCES AND ANGLICAN CHURCHES

Moravian Province	Anglican Church
Alaska	Episcopal Church in the USA
America (North)	Episcopal Church in the USA
America (South)	Episcopal Church in the USA
Costa Rica	Episcopal Church in the USA
Honduras	Episcopal Church in the USA
Nicaragua	Episcopal Church in the USA
Britain	Church of England
	Church of Ireland
Continental European	Church of England
	(also Episcopal Church in the USA)
Czech Republic	Church of England
Eastern West Indies	Church in the Province of the West Indies
Jamaica	Church in the Province of the West Indies
Guyana	Episcopal Anglican Church of Brazil
Labrador	Anglican Church of Canada
South Africa	Church of the Province of Southern Africa
Tanzania (Rukwa)	Church of the Province of Tanzania
Tanzania (Southern)	Church of the Province of Tanzania
Tanzania (South Western)	Church of the Province of Tanzania
Tanzania (Western)	Church of the Province of Tanzania

Unity Undertakings:

North India	Church of North India (united church)
Star Mountain, Ramallah	Episcopal Church in Jerusalem and the Middle East

Note: The Moravian Province of Surinam does not fall within the area of any Anglican church.